Playa Works   Environmental Arts and Humanities Series

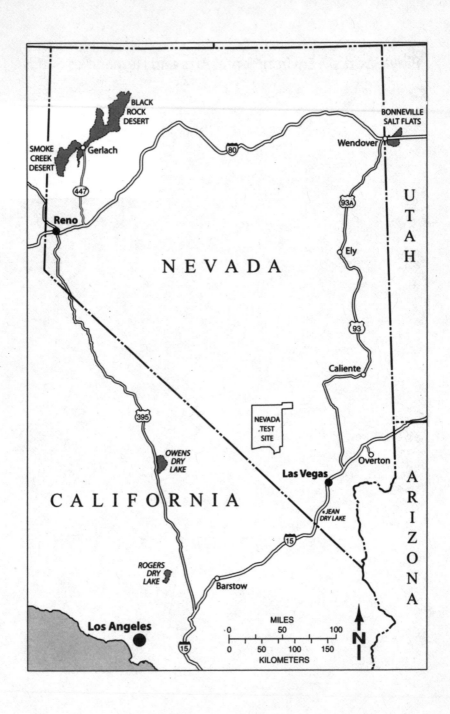

William L. Fox **Playa Works** The Myth of the Empty

UNIVERSITY OF NEVADA PRESS ▲▲ RENO & LAS VEGAS

Winner of the Wilbur S. Shepperson Humanities Book Award for 2002

This book is the recipient of the Wilbur S. Shepperson Humanities Book Award,
which is given annually in his memory by the Nevada Humanities Committee
and the University of Nevada Press. One of Nevada's most distinguished histori-
ans, Wilbur S. Shepperson was a founding member and long-time supporter of
both organizations.

This publication is made possible in part through generous grants from the
Nevada Humanities Committee, a state program of the National Endowment
for the Humanities and Furthermore Grants in Publishing, a program of
the J. M. Kaplan Fund.

Environmental Arts and Humanities Series

Series Editor: Scott Slovic

University of Nevada Press, Reno, Nevada 89557 USA

Copyright © 2002 by University of Nevada Press

All rights reserved

Manufactured in the United States of America

Design by Carrie House

Frontispiece: Map by Kris Pizarro

Library of Congress Cataloging-in-Publication Data
Fox, William L. (William Lyman), 1940–
Playa works : the myth of the empty / William L. Fox.
p. cm. — (Environmental arts and humanities series)
Includes bibliographical references.
ISBN 0-87417-523-2 (hardcover : alk. paper)
1. Southwest, New—Description and travel. 2. Nevada—
Description and travel. 3. Southwest, New—History,
Local. 4. Playas—Southwest, New. 5. Landscape—Social
aspects—Southwest, New. 6. Landscape—Southwest,
New—Psychological aspects. 7. Natural history—South-
west, New. 8. Southwest, New—In art. 9. Fox, William L.
(William Lyman), 1940—Journeys—Southwest, New.
I. Title. II. Series.
F787 .F695 2002
979—dc21   2002004784

The paper used in this book meets the requirements of
American National Standard for Information Sciences—
Permanence of Paper for Printed Library Materials, ANSI
Z39.48-1984. Binding materials were selected for strength
and durability.

ISBN 978-1-64779-153-7 (paper)

This book has been reproduced as a digital reprint.

Contents

Illustrations

Acknowledgments

Several people at the University of Nevada, Reno (UNR) have lent their intellectual capital to *Playa Works*. When describing to Scott Slovic at UNR's Center for Environmental Arts and Humanities in 1998 how the arc of my writing was proceeding through deserts of the world, including the Antarctic, he pointed out to me that I seemed to be formulating an arid-land aesthetic, an insight typical of Scott's generosity and in part responsible for this book. His colleagues Cheryll Glotfelty, Mike Branch, and Michael Cohen have also encouraged my work.

Dr. Robert Solso at the UNR Department of Psychology, author of *Cognition and the Visual Arts,* waited patiently below me with a safety net every time I climbed out on the limb of the cognitive sciences. My speculations in that arena, however, remain solely my responsibility.

Bob Blesse, who runs both Special Collections at the UNR Library and the Black Rock Press, has been a supportive colleague for two decades, which has often translated into awards from the Hilliard Foundation to assist with travel. I also want to thank Cheryl Taylor, formerly of the Nevada Historical Society, and Jim McCormick, formerly the chair of the UNR Art Department and the founder of the ongoing Nevada Artists Registry Project, for their research into the history of the visual arts in the state.

Derek Scammel, at the Department of Energy in Las Vegas, has been a knowledgeable guide to the Nevada Test Site for many years. Jim Graham, one of the media people for Burning Man, provided excellent coordination with that organization. Mike Bilbo in the Winnemucca office of the Bureau of Land Management likewise was generous with information about the Black Rock Desert and the permitting process for Burning Man. The geomorphologist Barbara Bilbo helped straighten out some of the geology of playas.

The University of Nevada Press has been a publisher of two of my previous books, and Margaret Dalrymple, formerly its editor-in-chief, agreed to a request to continue as my editor with grace and elan. Ron Latimer, director of the press, Carrie House, their talented designer, and Christine Campbell in marketing have also provided close support.

I can never get through one of these acknowledgments without thanking Alvin McLane, who continues to drag me across playas, through sand dunes and rock gardens, and up peaks of varying dimensions. He is quite solely responsible for my obsession with the desert, though I cannot hold him or anyone else responsible for any mistakes I may commit either outdoors or in *Playa Works*. Tom Radko, my close friend and agent, shores up the other end of my writing life with humor and goodwill.

The Myth of the Empty   An Introduction

When I told a Chilean artist friend that I was going to write a book about what people do on the playas of Nevada, he tilted his head to the right, squinted, and asked how was I going to do that in the desert. *Playa* in Spanish means beach or shore. Did it mean something different in English?

No, I replied, that's what it means, but we apply the word to those lake beds in the desert that are more often dry than wet.

Mauricio Arboleda smiled and nodded. A painter working in Las Vegas, he understood perfectly how parts of the desert form a palimpsest, a surface we draw upon time and time again, each message eventually erased by the elements to offer up an almost blank slate. They are a landlocked kind of beach, a geological shoreline onto which water runs from the sky and nearby mountains and, having no escape, then evaporates or soaks into the ground. A playa is an anti-oasis. When clay playas get wet, the sediments swell and refuse to accept moisture; the water evaporates. Playas with sandy bottoms just leak it away. In either case, the waters disappear, leaving behind a salt or alkali flat, a perpetual *tabula rasa* upon which the marks of people also wash up and then disappear. A playa is the absolute visual sink in the core of the void, a white hole into which our imaginations vanish.

I say that the playas are "almost" erased, for although we don't always see physical traces of the previous messages, they do exist, in our memories if nowhere else. We codify what we have done on the playas in history, in literature, and in art. Playas have been mined for salt, starting in the Sahara at least two thousand years ago, an activity that continues there and elsewhere today, as in the western United States. Although you can't grow crops on their highly mineralized and salt surfaces, playas often cover important groundwater resources that are tapped by nearby farms, and in Texas they've been used for recreational fishing when wet. We erect movie sets on them for westerns, horror flicks, and science-fiction films, since nothing else exists there to contradict the reality we wish to construct.

We photograph fashion models out on the playas, where the white ground is a perfect foil to the bright figure of desire. Land-speed records, another fashionable form of lust, can be broken nowhere else but on a playa, the flattest surfaces on the planet, and advertisements for automobiles trail along, the commercial corollary to the sport of engineering. The military and its industrial partners in aerospace manufacturing value playas not only as logistical flats but also for their strategic remoteness, using them as sites upon which to test experimental aircraft. Area 51 within the Nellis Air Range was chosen in 1955 for exactly those characteristics, being located on the Groom and Papoose Lake playas. Edwards Air Force Base, where the space shuttle is diverted when the weather deteriorates at Cape Canaveral, uses yet another Mojave playa for a landing strip.

The word itself was first applied in a scientific context by G. K. Gilbert in 1875, in his report on the geology of the American West as inspected during the federal survey west of the 100th meridian; he didn't bother defining it for his audience, so presumably by that time it was already in widespread use. Ten years later, we get a clue to the origin of its usage from the geologist Israel C. Russell, who noted that when the ephemeral lakes dried out they left behind wind-rippled mud that looked like a shoreline. Mauricio's understanding of the word wasn't far off, at all.

In the terms of a limnologist, or scientist specializing in lakes, a playa is an intracontinental basin wherein the balance of water falls into the negative. To form, a playa must reside within an area where evaporation greatly exceeds precipitation, often at a rate of ten times to one. There must be no outward drainage so all the silts deposit evenly and with regularity over great periods of time. Playas usually get wet on at least a semiregular basis, and sheets of water only a few inches thick may stand on them for varying periods of time before disappearing. While the water is there, it's pushed around by wind, sometimes traveling up to four feet per minute and polishing the surface as it goes—water that then freezes in winter, the wind mobilizing sheets of ice that also burnish the ground. When drying out, the playas crack into irregular patterns, often unsorted polygons derived from the molecular structure of clay, and daily freeze-thaw cycles pry apart individual grains of sand and silt. Wind shovels the fugitive particles around, further sanding down any marks made earlier on the surface, whether it was during the previous summer, or last week.

As many as fifty thousand playas may exist around the world, most of them less than a few square miles in size, perhaps fewer than a thousand covering sixty square miles or more. In Southwest Africa, they're called *vlor* (dry lake) or *kalahari* (salt lake); in North Africa *choot, sebka, merdja;* in the Middle East, *shott;* in Asia, *nor, sebehet, schala.* Russians refer to them as *pliazh,* Iranians as *kewire.* In Chile, they can be *salar* when they contain much salt, or *salina* when salt is only barely present. Australians differentiate their playas into *salt pans, boinka,* and *salina.* Most of the classic American playas are remnants of prehistoric desert lakes that have existed intermittently during wet, or pluvial, intervals of the previous 1.8 million years.

I say "classic," a decidedly nontechnical term, because this book takes place among the playas of the Great Basin and the Mojave deserts of the American Southwest, which fit the above description. These are among the most-studied playas in the world, and the dry lakes that most inhabit our imagination. However, as scientists have had increasing opportunities to study the country's surface from airplanes and satellites, it has become obvious that the definition can be applied to millions of other dry lakes. For instance, the High Plains of northwestern Texas and surrounding states contain 25,000 wind-dished catchments—in places packed as densely as one per square mile—that are technically playas. But because they leak water downward into the underlying Ogallala Aquifer, hence don't exist in a hydrologically closed system, they're classified as "recharge playas." If that's not stretching things enough, consider that these intermittently flooded basins, which are sometimes referred to as playa lakes, are critical habitats for waterfowl and are governed by the federal government as wetlands.

In the northern Great Plains of the United States and western Canada, there are somewhere between 1.5 million and a staggering 10 million ponds and small lakes that fill with water during the wet season, only to empty through evaporation during the autumnal dry season. So numerous that they remain uncounted, they, too, are considered playas by limnologists. Despite the importance of these features to local and regional ecosystems, they fall outside of what the public imagination considers the typical playa, which is that much larger and sometimes metaphorical void found in the West.

The greatest concentration of pluvial lakes in the Western Hemisphere lies within the Great Basin Desert of North America, an inward-draining bowl that encompasses 165,000 square miles of Nevada and western Utah. During the late Pleistocene, as many as 120 of them formed within the rain shadows cast by mountain ranges, existing in the past not so much because of greater precipitation but because evaporation was less than now. The pluvial lakes often received the majority of their water as runoff from those nearby mountains, as do their occasionally moist playa remnants, the latter thus highly susceptible to changes in climate. Playas undergo radical swings from dry to wet conditions within hours, and can cycle in and out of existence through periods that can range from daily to monthly to millennial.

Most of the thirty-nine major playas of the Great Basin were once interconnected as part of two immense Pleistocene lakes. Sixteen thousand years ago, the larger, Lake Bonneville in Utah, was a thousand feet deep and covered nearly 20,000 square miles—almost the size of Lake Michigan—before it cut a cataclysmic escape channel to the north. Nevada's Lake Lahontan, at its largest around 13,800 years ago, though smaller, still covered 8,665 square miles. It reached its deepest, nine hundred feet, where Pyramid Lake sits today, just north of Reno. You could have rowed a boat from a hundred miles southeast of Reno northward to almost the Idaho border, nearly two hundred miles, and east to Elko. Just for historical comparison, the Great Salt

Lake, the larger remnant of the two ancient lakes, today covers an average of 2,400 square miles, and at its historical low in 1964 extended over only 940 square miles and was nowhere deeper than twenty-six feet.

The largest playa, and therefore one of the largest flat places in the world, may be Lake Eyre in Australia, which has a surface area of 3,600 square miles. Its playa filled up for the first time in recorded history in 1950 with a thin layer of water and took two years to dry out again. Formed by a sagging of the continent's surface, which puts the playa currently forty feet below sea level, its pluvial lake once covered 40,000 square miles. The largest playa in North America is the Great Salt Lake Desert in Utah; the second is the Black Rock Desert of Northern Nevada. The latter has been classified as an "absolute desert," nothing lives permanently atop its 400-square-mile surface, and only a few invertebrate species are thought to survive below it during the intense summers.

How flat are playas? As the flattest natural features on earth, the elevation of a playa may change only inches over many miles; topographical maps of the Black Rock Desert and other playas, such as the Carson Sink, sometimes carry only a single one-foot contour line within the approximately sixty square miles of the entire sheet. As a result of sitting within enclosed basins and undergoing cyclical flooding, playas tend to be surrounded by enormous bathtub rings—ancient shorelines, terraces, wave-cut cliffs, and strandlines that are visible from miles away. When standing in the middle of a small circular playa, you feel as if you're occupying the center of a concentric target. If the depth of the water on a flooded playa increases by only a few inches, the temporary lake can grow by hundreds of square miles; deepen it a foot or two, and the coverage increases again, but by a factor of ten. Along much of your imaginary boat journey to Elko, you would have been stirring up bottom mud with your oars.

Today, playas in much of the world are growing in size and number, in the American West not so much from a drying of the climate as from the prodigious pumping of groundwater for agricultural purposes. One of the telltale symptoms is an increase in the dessication fissures that form on their surfaces, cracks that may be only a few inches in length and depth or up to three feet wide and fifty feet deep, creating enormous interlocking polygons up to a thousand feet across, features so large they were undiscovered until the application of aerial photography to playas in the 1950s, when the military surveyed them as likely candidates for airstrips.

You would think that playas are mostly devoid of history, but they aren't, and sometimes for surprising reasons. It's difficult to know what might have occurred on the flats of the Great Basin before the widespread use of that written record we label history, since mud and sand accumulate in the waters, then tend to bury any physical traces as the playas dry out. Nearby caves that were inhabited or used for storage over thousands of years, and that have been excavated by archaeologists, however, yield evidence to the cultures that depended on the existence of the pluvial lakes as a resource. Rock rings around the shorelines, as well as prehistoric fishhooks and small spear points, indicate that people fished the lakes when they existed, but much of the material culture from earlier inhabitants of the Great Basin was made from reeds growing near the water and other perishable organic substances.

North of Hazen, the remnant of a railroad town that sits near the juncture of Interstate 80 and Nevada State Highway 50, there is a micro-playa about 405 feet in diameter, one of the thousands of such tiny enclosed basins within the boundaries of the larger region. And encircling almost half of its circumference is a serpentine line of black volcanic stones running 685 feet around the rim of the white surface. Or, rather, that was the case in late 1996 when Alvin McLane, the legendary field guide, first saw it. Alvin, who has recorded more rock-art sites in Nevada than anyone else, came back the following January to map the site and photograph it, but by the time we returned in September 2000 more than 180 feet of the geoglyph—a figure drawn on the ground by laying down rocks—had disappeared. The stones had been removed to the center of the playa where they had been rearranged to form the names and initials of locals traversing the area. The mound of rocks forming the head of the serpentlike form was still intact, though its center had obviously been disturbed by artifact seekers at an earlier time, but the end of the tail was being recycled into graffiti.

An hour's drive to the north, on twin micro-playas that lie west of the navy's illegal Bravo 20 bombing range on the Forty Mile Desert, the tiny northern basin of these two playas holds a seventy-foot-long anthropomorph, arms outstretched with its feet standing in what might be taken for lines of water. The mounds at both its head and the terminus of its right arm have been dug up, raided by people seeking the artifacts accompanying prehistoric burials.

Geoglyphs are the rarest, least-studied, and most inscrutable of all rock-art forms. Calling them "art" is, in fact, to attribute only our modern interpretation to ancient manipulations of the earth's surface that may have had more to do with religion and social mechanics. But the geoglyphs of the Northern Nevada playas demonstrate that we have used those blank surfaces to receive human meaning for upwards of at least six thousand years. Despite the geoglyphs, however, most of what we know of activity on the playas dates only from the mid-nineteenth century onward.

By the 1860s, for instance, both the Great Salt Lake and Black Rock playas had been crossed by tens of thousands of settlers who followed the emigrant trails to California, trails first established by Indians, then fur trappers and a few hardy explorers. Jim Bridger and Étienne Provost separately discovered the Great Salt Lake in the mid-1820s, and that most redoubtable of all scouts, Jedediah Smith, actually crossed the Great Basin twice in 1827, on his return trip becoming the first Euro-American to traverse central Nevada. In all probability, Smith divined the enclosed nature of the region and knew that no legendary river, such as the hypothetical Rio San Buenaventura, flowed westward out of it.

Unfortunately, Smith was killed and his maps were lost before he could add much to the cartographic record; as late as 1840, David Burr, geographer to the U.S. House of Representatives, could only quote Smith's description of the Great Basin as a "Great Sandy Plain" on his official map of the country. It wouldn't be until John Charles Frémont, led by Kit Carson and accompanied by the grumbling but meticulous German cartographer Charles Preuss, circumnavigated the basin on his second journey through the West that the true nature of the last geophysical province in North America to be discovered would begin to become apparent and the cartographic grid drawn accurately across even a small portion of it.

Frémont and his men ventured out onto the Black Rock Desert in late December 1843, searching for the mythical San Buenaventura, a river that supposedly flowed west out of the Rockies to the Pacific Ocean. They never located the fabled watercourse and instead found their horses going lame on ground that was alternately fine sand, sticky clay, and sharp rocks. On January 2, 1844, Frémont noted that the "rocks are volcanic, and the hills here have a burnt appearance— cinders and coal occasionally appearing as at a blacksmith's forge." That night, a fog rose up from the playa that was so heavy the men sent out to harness the horses became lost and disoriented. Frémont fretted that "the appearance of the country was so forbidding, that I was afraid to enter it." The fog lasted for several days, and the party wandered along ridges bordering the playa, slowly using up their water and livestock feed, until Frémont did what he was always inclined to do, climb the nearest peak. Dragging Preuss behind them, he and Carson were able to get high enough to see steam rising above the fog from the hot springs near present-day Gerlach.

By April of that year, having escaped the Great Basin by making a characteristically ill-advised and almost fatal crossing of the Sierra Nevada in midwinter, Frémont's expedition was headed east across the Mojave region of the Great Basin, where he was warned by Indians that on the playas "there is neither water nor grass—nothing; every animal that goes out upon them, dies." The following month, his 3,500-mile exploration completed, he officially concluded that there was no San Buenaventura River, that the Great Basin was a single enclosed entity, and that "sterility may be its prominent characteristic." He compared the region to Asia, where other interior continental basins were known to exist "in that ancient quarter of the globe," thus deliberately evoking a sense of the mysterious in the minds of his readers.

Preuss, however, had kept track of the geography with his two barometric altimeters, sextants, and numerous compasses, and his maps in the expedition account published the year after their return provided a ready guide for what would soon be a mass migration to California. It is recorded that 250 people crossed the Great Basin in 1845; three years later, up to 25,000 were crossing Nevada on their way to the California gold mines. How they perceived the playas as they crossed them amounted to nothing less than a mass hallucination.

The playas were dry and hot, but the wagonmasters welcomed their firm surfaces and flatness after threading the way across the Rockies and through the Wasatch Range of Utah—and the playas offered the most direct passage across the Great Basin. There was a severe downside to the playa crossings, however. The bleak and forbidding flats that had almost defeated experienced travelers such as Frémont and Carson proved totally dispiriting to novice emigrants. The Forty Mile Desert in Nevada—a series of flats and playas extending south of the Humboldt River to just north of Fallon (a town on what is now labeled "the loneliest road in America")—was the deadliest part of the entire emigrant trail. More graves there than anywhere else marked the toll taken by the hyper-arid environment, as did the bloated carcasses of dead livestock and increasingly large heaps of cast-off household goods. Bits of rust from abandoned tools and wagon parts can still be found occasionally along the route, though history buffs and scavengers with metal detectors have mostly cleaned up every old trail in the West.

Firsthand accounts from the emigrants leave no doubt that they misperceived the desert and the playas in two distinct ways: they couldn't see them as places where people could exist, and they consistently underestimated the distances involved. Both perceptions led them to lose heart, and sometimes their will to live. The reason they saw the desert in such terms was not that they were naïve or unschooled; it sits deeper within the evolution of human neurophysiology, which in turn has everything to do with why the art and other marks we create on and about the playas look they way they do.

The earliest known views of Great Basin playas were sketches and maps made by artists and surveyors accompanying the army and railroad surveys of the West in the mid-nineteenth century. Frémont took a daguerreotype camera with him on both his first and second expeditions, but he failed to use the device successfully; the camera would not make a successful appearance on the playas until the mid-1860s with the advent of Timothy O'Sullivan, who made views across the entire Great Basin with the Clarence King expedition of 1867–1869. Frémont's report from his second expedition was published in 1845, and although it painted vivid literary images of the playas and included a shaded relief map of the Great Salt Lake and a sketch of Pyramid Lake by Preuss, it didn't contain pictorial representations of the playas. Howard Stansbury's report of his survey of the Great Salt Lake came out in 1852, and it includes numerous lithographs of the lake and surrounding landscape, but no playa pictures.

The first actual picture of a playa may be the wide panoramic lithograph that unfolds out of the 1861 Pacific Railroad survey. *Valley of the Mud Lakes* depicts the Smoke Creek and Black Rock playas and covers more than eighty miles from end to end; across the deserts in clear detail stand peaks ninety miles distant from each other. You can recognize every feature on the horizon today, so accurate is the work. The artist, F. W. von Egloffstein, was careful to include in it a figure with his horse, perhaps Lieutenant E. G. Beckwith, leader of the expedition, as well as a flock of birds in the all-but-empty sky. The figures provide scale and anchor our gaze, which would otherwise fall off the page, so little is there to hold onto in most of the picture.

The panorama illustrates the perceptual problems faced by emigrants in the Forty Mile Desert and on playas elsewhere. We're animals that evolved in adaptation to our original environment of forest and rolling woodlands in the African savanna that existed throughout the Pleistocene, an epoch that lasted from 1.6 million years to about 10,000 years ago. Eighty percent of the sensory information we take in comes through our vision. The hardware of our eyes, and more importantly the software of our minds, were wired and programmed by hundreds of thousands, if not millions of years of living and dying in a specific visual landscape. Hence, we do well in spaces that are broken into a foreground with trees or other strong verticals behind which we can protect ourselves while looking about. We like a long vista with trees of a similar size interspersed throughout, which helps us tell how far things are and provides refuge as we move through the land. And we prefer water somewhere in the midground of our view, a place to quench our thirst and find game.

We're used to, and expect, enough moisture in the air so that light scatters in predictable ways, making the far hills turn blue with what painters label "atmospheric perspective." Our bodies know that vegetation is green, that temperatures usually swing only twenty or so degrees from day to night, and that if we follow water downstream, we'll probably find more of our kind. We've codified this knowledge in everything from European landscape painting to the Boy Scout Handbook—and it all fails us out here in the arid West.

The humidity in North America's four deserts—the Great Basin, the Mojave, the Sonoran, and the Chihuahuan—is so low that a color shift in the air may not occur within twenty miles, much less the two or three to which we're accustomed in more temperate places. And ridgelines miles away, which should be softened across the distance, remain as clear as picture postcards or a topographical panorama.

Trees are nonexistent on the playas, which around their edges host low plants spaced relatively far apart and of a modest gray-green appearance, adaptations to scarce rainfall and the high angle of the sun. The contours are unfamiliar, and we find nothing of significant vertical size in the fore- or middle ground to give us a sense of size, distance, or scale. We have no trees or buildings to hide behind, from which to progress one to another in security across the land. So few of the directional cues exist on the largest playas that, if you close your eyes while walking, you'll travel in a circle. In fact, open your eyes and keep walking. Unless you keep strict track of the angle of your shadow and compensate for the changing position of the sun, you'll still find yourself walking in a circle.

We're accustomed to finding the horizon across an unobstructed flat surface, assuming our eyes are five feet above the ground, about 2.8 statute miles away. We see a world that lies within a circumscribed area of roughly 31 square miles. On a medium-sized playa within the Great Basin, the mountains might rise up three or four miles on either side of you, and you'll perceive yourself to be standing in the middle of 64 square miles; in larger valleys, the vista can expand up to 1,800 square miles. In the middle of a playa, we can see other human figures only within about a mile of us. Farther away than that, they're invisible. We look around us and cannot but fail to understand how large the space is.

Then there is the matter of the mirage—those discontinuities of temperature in the air that bend and transmit light in ways that are mathematically predictable but counterintuitive to our evolved perceptual means. What looks like a lake may be nothing but a reflection of the sky bounced from the boundary between hot and cool air, or of a lake that lies in reality beyond the horizon, a vision projected in front of us by a happenstance of convection.

When you get results completely out of alignment with your perceptual expectations, it's called cognitive dissonance. As a result of this perceptual dislocation, emigrants of the nineteenth century and tourists in the twenty-first alike made and continue to make bad judgment calls. People still insist on taking walks into the desert with preparations based on what they *think* the distances look like, versus what they *are*. This means they sometimes run out of water and die of thirst ... or heatstroke ... or hunger.

We have developed various visual aids to help us cope with our cognitive dissonance in isotropic landscapes—those places where similar features are distributed evenly across large spaces. The cartographic grid is one, the imposition of a regularly spaced imaginary set of lines over the desert allowing us to measure it off in ways we understand, and from which we can calculate how much water we'll really need. Frémont brought the altimeter and Teutonic precision with him in 1843–1844; Howard Stansbury, another army topographical engineer, established the use of triangulation in the West for the first time with his survey of the Great Salt Lake during 1849–1850. Without all three—accurate elevations, measured baselines, and consistent precision—it would have been impossible even to begin to establish our position on the playas and thus understand how wide the gap is between our perceptions and the reality. The annual Burning Man celebration, which puts upwards of twenty thousand people out on the Black Rock playa, issues stern warnings to participants about the dissonance and how to avoid its effects. People still don't get it and die.

Our dissonance in an extreme landscape produces more than a basic survival need to measure and cope. We're also driven to understand, to make images of and represent it, as if we don't fully possess a place until we understand what it means. The primary way we try to understand the playas, apart from drilling cores in them and measuring their chemical composition, is by making art on and about them. Preuss and Egloffstein with their maps and sketches were just the beginning.

Finally, a word about deserts, the larger geographical context of the playas. Arid and semiarid lands together comprise a third of the planet's total land surface. Deserts, often defined as arid lands that receive less than ten inches of rain a year, cover approximately eight million square miles of the earth. Their precipitation can range from virtually zero in the Atacama of Peru to more than eleven inches in the Sonoran Desert of Arizona and northern Mexico. They mostly occur along the Tropic of Cancer in the Northern Hemisphere and the Tropic of Capricorn in the Southern, or between the 15th and 35th degrees of the horse latitudes—which means they have in common high atmospheric pressure and dry winds that have dropped their moisture while warm in the tropical latitudes and have since cooled as they spread out toward the poles, thus losing some of their ability to hold moisture. The character of these winds is not so much to bring moisture to the land as to actually bear it away; evaporation has as much to do with creating and maintaining aridity as the lack of rainfall.

Deserts tend to be inland from the ocean or to sit within rain shadows caused by mountains or cold ocean currents, factors that further dry the air, and temperature is not the causative factor one might think: the world's largest arid region is the 5.4-million-square-mile Antarctic, which receives a continental average of only five to six inches of precipitation annually. The largest and fiercest desert on the planet, in fact, is the East Antarctic Plateau, where recorded temperatures have fallen to -129°F, more than one hundred sixty degrees of frost. On the other end of the scale, summer air temperatures have hovered around 135°F in both Africa's Libyan Desert and in our own Death Valley.

The territory covered by *Playa Works* includes the largest and coldest of the North American deserts, the Great Basin, where snow in the winter is frequent; and the smallest and hottest, the adjacent Mojave, where temperatures routinely soar above 120°F within those 550 square miles of Death Valley that are below sea level. The mountains of the Great Basin rise to over 13,000 feet; the lowest point in the Western Hemisphere is 282 feet below sea level in Death Valley, where it rains about 1.6 inches per year.

The combined surface area of the four North American deserts is only about 500,000 square miles, the fifth largest nonpolar desert on the planet. Lest we be too impressed, the Sahara in Africa is seventy times larger, 3.5 million square miles. Next in size is the Australian desert at 1.3 million square miles. Many deserts worldwide, however, are growing, as are the semiarid lands, which cover an equivalent area. Whereas in the past both have shrunk or enlarged primarily because of climatic changes, increasingly it is clear that human usage has become a major factor in their spread.

Desertification, which refers specifically to the process by which humans degrade soils and vegetative covers through abuse and overuse—through overgrazing and groundwater pumping, for example—now claims 77,000 square miles of agricultural land worldwide each year. The International Soil Reference and Information Centre in the Netherlands estimates that we have degraded more than 17 percent of the earth's land surface since the end of World War II in 1945, and that 3.7 *billion* acres of topsoil are eroded each year. It's estimated that a sixth of the world's population already lives in or is reliant upon resources derived from the deserts themselves—a figure projected to rise to as high as 50 percent by the middle of this century. A statistic close to home is that the population of the American desert Southwest is projected to increase by 40 percent from 2001 to 2025.

The separation of deserts and desertified lands is useful for scientists measuring our effects on the planet, but it's perhaps an increasingly difficult distinction to make, not least because nature is not an either/or proposition existing apart from us. Our species now warms the global climate, which in turn is increasing rainfall in some areas and decreasing it in others. And sometimes deserts and desertification are spiraled upward through our actions, such as in the Aral Sea of Central Asia.

Located in or on the borders of three countries formerly in the Soviet Union—Uzbekistan, Turkmenistan, and Tajikistan—at 26,000 square miles the Aral Sea was once the fourth largest freshwater lake in the world. It had been shrinking slowly since the end of the Pleistocene, but in the early 1950s the Soviet government decided to increase dramatically the production of cotton upstream from the Aral. In 1954, the 805-mile-long Kara Kum Canal was built, initiating a large-scale diversion of the rivers feeding the Aral, which was necessary to irrigate the water-intensive crops upstream. As a result, the Aral has shrunk by more than 50 percent in the last forty years, its shoreline receding up to fifty miles in some places. Now the Kara Kum ("Black Sands") and Kyzyl Kum ("Red Sands") deserts meet on its bed. The Aral is on its way to becoming one of the world's largest playas.

What does such an immense desertification mean? First, it has itself changed the regional climate, making it hotter in the summer and colder in the winter, and drier all year long, a synergy that hastens the degradation. Second, it means that around 75 million tons of dust now blow off the dry lakebed to cover surrounding lands, and salts from the Aral blow as far away as Belarus, six hundred miles to the northwest. The airborne dust contains metals such as lead and zinc, which has led to a fivefold increase in anemia during the last decade; 97 percent of all women in the surrounding Karakalpakstan Republic are afflicted, their ability to absorb iron into their blood severely diminished. The insecticide DDT, which is still being sprayed on crops upstream, is also in the air, as is strontium that settled in the sediments during the atomic testing conducted in the 1950s and 1960s. Liver cancer is up 200 percent, infant mortality 20 percent. Chronic bronchitis has increased 3,000 percent in fifteen years, arthritic diseases 6,000 percent.

The Aral Sea may disappear in as soon as fifteen years. The Food and Agriculture Organization of the United Nations, which supplied these figures, worries that the 1.2 million residents of the republic are being so decimated by these environmental effects that their country as a geopolitical entity may simply cease to exist. Much the same dynamics are at work on Lake Chad in central North Africa, which has shrunk from 9,700 square miles in 1963 to less than 580 square miles in 2001.

Reyner Banham, a twentieth-century aficionado of the Mojave, noted in his modern classic, *Scenes in America Deserta,* that *desert* traditionally means a place that is deserted, without people, unpopulated, but perhaps closer to the truth is that deserts are places where people are merely less frequent than elsewhere. He concluded: "The ultimate definition of a true desert may yet prove to be concerned with the number and type of people present, and what they think they are doing there."

Deserts are not empty. Almost always they are occupied by plants, though distributed sparsely, and are prowled by animals and insects of many kinds, which tend to come out after the sun goes down. Deserts often exist between more moderate environments and thus become places constantly crossed by people going from one place to another, which is most definitely the case for those American deserts next to the Mediterranean environs of California.

Deserts are also what we take to be transformative spaces. If we suffer in our contact with them from a cognitive dissonance that can kill us, the dislocation of our senses in deserts also provides an opportunity to experience a different way of relating to the world. If the lack of visual cues leads to our walking in a circle, it can also dramatically increase our haptic, or whole-body, perception of the landscape. In the desert you can feel as if, by being radically diminished in size, you are more properly scaled to the planet. It seems as if your mind expands to fill the space around you, an eerie and very nearly hallucinogenic experience, and one probably related to why so many religions, in particular monotheisms, were birthed in the deserts of the Middle East.

Deserts are where people strive to make and leave a mark, especially on those most barren portions of them, the playas. While the floors of the desert valleys in the Mojave and the Great Basin are not usually flat themselves, nor devoid of vegetation, the playas are. Sometimes the marks we make on playas are targets painted on the flats for pilots to aim at as they practice bombing runs; sometimes the marks are paintings by artists. Sometimes the two are almost indistinguishable from each other. Parsing out why that is so allows us to learn about how we function in those large and empty spaces in which we are increasingly living, which is a matter of importance.

A Tour of the Playa   Part I: The Mojave

The Center for Land Use Interpretation occupies the east end of a nondescript commercial building at 9331 Venice Boulevard in Culver City, part of the Greater Los Angeles metropolitan area. The other end of the building is taken up by that marvelous and eccentric creation of David Wilson, the Museum of Jurassic Technology. The museum exhibits things that almost should be, or in vague absurdity, actually are. Take, for instance, the stink ants of Cameroon and the artifacts of mobile-home parks. Both are offered with a deadpan commentary that leaves the viewer to decide if they're real or not, which is very much the point.

The CLUI, a nonprofit organization that catalogs sites of unusual land use and makes them accessible through visual documentation, likewise presents itself with a certain neutral view toward reality. When the Center mounted an exhibition of oblique aerial photographs by Bill DuBois of the open-pit gold mines in Nevada, for instance, the wall labels gave the locations and names of the mines alongside facts and figures about the industry and its methods, but took no stand regarding either the environmental or aesthetic effects of what were collectively titled "Monuments of Displacement." This practice sometimes frustrates environmental activists, but it gives the CLUI access to sites and materials that would otherwise be off limits.

Heap-leeching—the method of gold extraction currently used by the immense open-pit mines—involves tearing down entire mountains and rearranging them into giant heaps of tailings, which are then washed with a cyanide solution. The mixture percolates through the dirt, attaches itself to the microscopic gold within, and is then processed to remove the precious mineral. Much of the cyanide is recycled, but large settling ponds with tons of the poison, even when netted to keep out migratory waterfowl, still contaminate groundwater, leak into streams, and sterilize the surrounding earth.

To a miner, open-pit gold mines are exquisite examples of contemporary earthworks that provide jobs; to a federal banker, they are a strategic economic resource; to a jeweler, they are the bands on a watch. Personally, I have a problem with tearing down the horizons of my home state and permanently polluting its waterways for a shiny metal, 80 percent of which worldwide ends up in trinkets that people wear as decorative status symbols. The CLUI is the only place I know, however, where you can sit down with a mining engineer and enjoy the industrial sublime that he's captured in full color from his airplane. The Center leaves it up to viewers to frame their own judgments.

The CLUI maintains a library, an invaluable on-line Land Use Database, and several buildings on a former World War II airbase in Wendover, Utah, which is where the director of the organization, Matt Coolidge, and I are headed. Along the way we'll pass through the Mojave Desert, Las Vegas, the Nevada Test Site, and thus go by some of the best-known playas in the world, those that have been featured in westerns, science-fiction movies, and news stories about nuclear bombs. Matt is an aficionado of playas with an unusual attitude toward them. Just as the Center is open to exhibiting the aerial photography of a mine supervisor, so it also hosts residencies for artists in Wendover and supports art installations at various locations, among them the desert playas of California, Nevada, and Utah. As a "research organization dedicated to finding the common ground in issues of land use," the Center recognizes art as being on equal footing with military and industrial uses of the playas.

Matt, who was one of the founders of the CLUI in 1994, is an American who was born in Montreal on the last day of 1966 but was sent to school in Boston when he was fourteen. The son of a medieval history professor, and brother of Miles Coolidge, a well-known Los Angeles photographer, he earned a B.A. in environmental studies and an informal minor in contemporary art and film from Boston University in 1991. He first came to California while he was still in high school, working as a carpenter and a cook, among other jobs, and returned in 1992 thinking he would attend one of the art schools in Los Angeles. He never got around to it, instead cultivating what I consider to be,

given his background, a perfectly logical taste for the gothic industri-
alism of abandoned military installations and other examples of
"dead tech."

Living in part of an old fruit-packing plant in Piru, a tiny agricultural town north of the San Fernando Valley, he did odd jobs for students at the California Institute for the Arts (Cal Arts) while making
sculptural environments in boxes that had peepholes for viewing the
interiors. Assembled out of old machine parts and glowing tubes, they
were in essence miniaturized industrial landscapes. The sculptures
never really satisfied him, though, and he shifted his focus from objects to places once he realized that "there was enough stuff in the
world for re-contextualization without making new things."

The CLUI came into being as a nonprofit organization when Matt
and friends—who were involved in a diversity of post-college jobs
such as aerial photography, petroleum-industry parts supply, organic
farming, and commercial demolition—banded together to investigate
how humans were using landscape. It gave them a way to unite their
interests, as well as to attract others who were like-minded. Although
they incorporated originally in the Bay Area, the audience there
seemed determined to take them for an environmental group, which
was to miss the point. More geographers of the industrial and military
terra incognita than anything else, the organization found itself moving in next to the Museum of Jurassic Technology because a friend
who was doing database preparation for them had an office there.

When I relocated in 1996 to Los Angeles from the deserts of Nevada and New Mexico, the CLUI was one of the first organizations I
stumbled across in town. I spoke with Matt as early as 1998 about
writing something regarding the CLUI, and the occasion of this investigation into playas was an obvious opportunity. Matt was making an
April trip to check out conditions at Michael Heizer's earth sculpture
in southern Nevada, *Double Negative,* which he would be visiting a
few weeks later with students, as well as to restock the Wendover facility. Along the way, we'd pass those highly visible Mojave playas but

also spend a day among the dry lakes of the Nevada Test Site in order for Matt to revise the Center's guidebook to the facilities there.

Matt picks me up on a weekday morning in the lumbering one-ton CLUI van, a 1992 fleet model formerly belonging to the Los Angeles Metropolitan Water District. Painted white with diagonal red stripes on the back doors, a back-up warning beeper, and the round CLUI logo on the doors, the van displays a moderately official air that comes in handy when poking around governmental and industrial sites. Inside, the dashboard is a maze of electronic wires and plugs, a power inverter, the inevitable tape and CD players, and a Global Positioning Unit hooked into one of the three laptops onboard. It's running a set of seamless USGS topographical maps and plotting our position as we drive onto Interstate 10 and head east toward the Mojave Desert. Watching the red dot that represents the van as it climbs up the contour lines is, oddly enough, more disorienting at first than not; it's as if we're a pawn being moved through a computer game, as well as free agents driving across the landscape.

Yesterday morning, a vigorous low moved through, peppering us with rain, hail, high winds, and what the weather casters were cautiously labeling "tornadic events." People in L.A. have a hard time admitting that the area suffers from small tornadoes every year, despite the fact that millions of residents have witnessed funnel clouds and hundreds of structures have been shredded along hopscotching paths of destruction that bear a striking similarity to those in news footage from Kansas. Whatever the cause of our cognitive conflict between the image of paradise in LaLa-Land and the natural realities of earthquakes, fires, mudslides, and tornadoes, it is at times an attractive place to live. This morning, the air is still murky, however, and the mountains are hidden until we're almost in the pass.

Once we leave the basins of Greater Los Angeles, climbing first up between the San Gabriels on our left and the San Bernardino Mountains to the east, we descend gently into the Mojave Desert. When I was a college student in the L.A. area during the late 1960s and driving home to Reno north along U.S. 395, coming over the Cajon Pass was like surfacing from underneath the ocean. The fog, smog, smoke, and acid rain of the urban basins sank behind the mountains, which contained both the fetid atmosphere and the rampant development. No longer. Now the smog often blows over the mountains in waves that reach to Las Vegas and Phoenix, and the urban grid has metastasized into the desert. Strip malls and housing developments, immense apartment complexes and discount shopping centers are plopped down inside a familiar rectilinear pattern that self-replicates clear to Barstow, almost an hour away, before it begins to peter out.

But it's also in the Mojave where we find the playas with mass-media audiences. This is the most heavily traveled, studied, and documented desert in the world, because of its proximity to Hollywood and the universities of Los Angeles. It's what we conceive of as the archetypal model for a wasteland, the landscape of denial, tribulation, and rebirth. It's where we imagine men transforming into saints, whether in the Bible, Clint Eastwood movies, or the *Dune* novels of Frank Herbert and the Mars trilogy by Kim Stanley Robinson. It's no accident that Ray Bradbury, another author of classic Martian tales, is a Southern California native, or that Robinson grew up and attended college here. They had the Mojave to watch in films, to visit, to ponder as a blank stage upon which to set their epics of personal and planetary transformation. And it's where scientists go to examine the conditions under which life might actually exist on Mars, the playas of Death Valley being among the harshest environments on earth, akin to the Dry Valleys of the Antarctic—another desert used as an analog environment for scientific practice in the off-world.

The military controls five million acres on the Mojave and is always looking for more, a logistical need first claimed within weeks after the Japanese bombed Pearl Harbor at the start of World War II. The German general Erwin Rommel had arrived in Libya, and the Allies feared that he would blitzkrieg east across North Africa and capture the Suez Canal to join forces in Iraq with the Japanese, who were simultaneously chewing their way west across India. The American general George S. Patton was directed by the War Department to begin training troops for armored-vehicle warfare in the desert of Southern California, and he reconnoitered locations from the air, looking for proximity to both water and railroads. The Mojave was a logistician's dream come true, in relative proximity to Los Angeles with its airports, train depots, deepwater ports, and plenty of cheap land and labor for wartime production lines.

Patton fielded more than a million U.S. troops within the 18,000 square miles of the Desert Training Center (DTC), just to our north. He drilled up to two hundred thousand soldiers at a time, and sent out close to twenty thousand vehicles and aircraft throughout the arid valleys. The DTC spawned both Fort Irwin and the China Lake Naval Air Weapons Testing Center. The former is roughly the size of Rhode Island, and the tank tracks of Patton's men are still visible today; China Lake's million square acres have seen virtually every conventional munitions tested there.

Edwards Air Force Base, which contains Rogers and Rosamond Dry Lakes, is sited only a few valleys to the west and was used by the army as early as 1933 for a gunnery range. The playas of Edwards are exceptionally well suited to testing experimental aircraft; not only are they large—Rogers running forty-five miles square—but Rosamond offers less than eighteen inches of surface curvature along 30,000 feet. The first American jet aircraft were tested at Edwards; it provided the runway that Chuck Yeager used when breaking the sound barrier for the first time in 1947; and now it's the primary alternate landing site for the space shuttle.

The situation of the playas in the Mojave is thus a very mixed one. Those that are outside the military preserves, such as the El Mirage and Lucerne Dry Lakes, are now embedded in high-desert valley suburbs. Crossed by roads and surrounded by development, they no longer have the isolated grandeur that they once offered in the 1950s and 1960s, when the playas were Hollywood's backdrop for B-rated flicks about giant insects and motorcycle gangs invading small towns. The playas that are still pristine represent the desert as Stephen King and Steven Spielberg imagine it, the horror writer and the director themselves brought up on those same movies. It's the scenery that the fashion models in *Vogue* and *Elle* wear as if it were their outermost skin, a spare palette that shows to advantage their wan complexions, dramatic makeup, and the thin drapes of haute-couture designers. Nowadays, film crews, if they can afford it, go to Morocco where development is nonexistent—or at least, less intrusive—but car ads more often than not are still shot against the backdrop of the Mojave, the promise of an open road and throttle supposedly irresistible to young and affluent testosterone-laden American males.

On the other hand, the desert within the military preserves sometimes encompasses significant and healthy wilderness areas. Where the primary use is aerial, such as the navy's China Lake, pristine prehistoric rock-art sites and viable ecological habitats can coexist with the military. Land-based operations at places such as Fort Irwin tend to shred the desert. They destroy not only the sparse plant cover, but by raking up the natural desert pavement of gravel and lichens, churn vast acreage into wind-blown dust. All of the desert under military control, however, can be subjected to pollution, and as a result many of the playas in the West, while retaining much of their visual purity, are in reality often contaminated with toxic waste and unexploded munitions. The most vivid examples are, of course, within the Nevada Test Site, where what appear to be pristine flats are in a few places so invisibly radioactive with plutonium and other isotopes that they will remain deadly for tens of thousands of years.

The military has been known to inscribe its peculiar kinds of graphics on the desert floor, ranging from circular and rectilinear target patterns to what may be the largest compass rose in the world, a carto-graphic drawn on Rogers Dry Lake in order for pilots to get their bearings. This playa also hosts seven runways etched on its surface, the longest one of which extends for seven and a half miles. We can't help but think of other kinds of earthworks when we see photographs of these figures created on the ground but readable only from the air. Outside Blythe, a town near where I-10 crosses into Arizona, enormous sets of "intaglios" were drawn around A.D. 800 by people scraping away the dark oxidized gravel surface to expose light material underneath. The ninety-four-foot-tall anthropomorph there is of a size comparable to the figures made by similar means several hundred years earlier on the coastal plains of Peru by the Nazca culture. Made from roughly 100 B.C. through A.D. 700 on a plain 1,500 feet above sea level—a desert that receives virtually no measurable rainfall—the Nazca drawings cover a three-hundred-square-mile area; some of their lines extend for miles and were rediscovered in modern times only through aerial surveys.

We colloquially call these and other prehistoric images left on the land "rock art," but anthropologists note that we have few clues to decipher the intent behind them. Prayers for rain, hunting instructions, solar markers, and aids for spiritual descent into the underworld are among the possible and credible explanations; use as navigational devices for alien visitors is a noncredible idea often belabored by pop television shows and late-night radio talk-show hosts. The prehistoric peoples who created such desert works, from cave images of Pluvial times in the Sahara to the more recent geo- and petroglyphs of the Great Basin, mostly worked on or above the shorelines of the ancient lakes; all we can still discern on the playas are the rare geoglyphs, created after the waters receded.

Whatever the intent of these figures on the ground, they have consistently informed the work of contemporary artists working on the playas, starting with Michael Heizer (1944–), the person credited most often with the invention of earthworks as an art genre. The artist, who spent years traveling with his late father, noted Berkeley anthropologist Dr. Robert F. Heizer, lived in countries such as Peru and Bolivia while his parent studied native megaliths. As a young man, the

Compass rose, Edwards Air Force Base, Rogers Dry Lake. Center for Land Use Interpretation (CLUI Archive)

Bombing targets constructed by Lockheed Martin Corporation. Photo courtesy of United States Air Force

Radar target. Photo courtesy of United States Air Force

· **Simulated surface-to-air missile complex target.** Photo courtesy of United States Air Force

artist accompanied him on field trips to the deserts of Egypt and Nevada, and was intimately familiar with the groundbreaking work his father did on everything from the Olmec sites in the Yucatán to the rock art of the Great Basin. More than any other artist in recent memory, Heizer was schooled firsthand in the deep history of image making, not simply a European tradition spanning a handful of centuries.

After attending the San Francisco Art Institute briefly in the early 1960s, Michael Heizer moved to New York City where he continued to paint large hard-edged geometric figures, first on Masonite and then on canvas. In 1967, restless with the domination of the art scene by galleries and museums catering to a European-driven art-historical agenda, Heizer left New York and returned to the American West, anxious to develop a vocabulary more indigenous to the Americas. He began to execute drawings and sculpture directly on the ground, working in the Sierra Nevada above Lake Tahoe and then in the deserts of California and Nevada. As such, his works were not representations of landscape but art at first placed on, then carved into, and finally and utterly made out of land.

Prior to Heizer, it's difficult to find examples of people making contemporary art on the playas. The flat landforms weren't, in fact, even represented much in traditional art forms. Timothy O'Sullivan photographed a few in Northern Nevada while working on a government survey in the late 1860s, and Ansel Adams made some memorable images of them for a 1950 edition of Mary Austin's *The Land of Little Rain*, one picture from the Owens Valley showing a fractal foreground of dessication fissures with the Sierra Nevada in the background "breaking over a desert shore." Most early photos of the desert concentrated on the buildings and people, as if the ostensibly empty landscape was too daunting to contemplate, or simply of no interest.

Only a handful of early- and mid-twentieth-century painters, notably among them Maynard Dixon and Robert Caples—artists who lived in Nevada for parts of their careers—painted pictures of playas and dry lakes. Usually the salt and alkali flats were backdrops for horses and cowboys, as in the case of Dixon's early work, or idealized as a compositional element in a larger and surreal space for Caples, depictions that carried over into the movies. Perhaps the best intersection of film and playa that had occurred by the midcentury was in *The Misfits* (1961), a film written by Arthur Miller and directed by John Huston, wherein a recent divorcée, played by Marilyn Monroe, is introduced to a playa about twenty-five miles east of Carson City by Clark Gable, who plays an older cowboy smitten with her. Driven out by Gable onto the dry lake to chase down wild horses, Monroe proclaims: "It's like a dream!"

Early in 1962, the Swiss sculptor Jean Tinguely (1925–1991) came to Las Vegas to construct and then destroy one of his famous "poetry in motion" sculptures. The already famous thirty-six-year-old artist combed the city dump for old refrigerators, bicycle wheels, air-conditioning units, and shopping carts, fusing them together in the parking lot of the Flamingo Hotel into improbable and gawky assemblages. At night, he sat in the hotel room with his collaborator, Niki de Saint-Phalle, and built bombs out of one hundred sticks of dynamite, an activity that Las Vegans would probably frown upon nowadays; in the decade when mushroom clouds from aboveground nuclear tests were visible from swimming pools outside the casinos, things were a little more casual.

After three weeks of intense work, Tinguely and Saint-Phalle lined up their seven sculptures in a row out on the Jean Dry Lake playa, just ten minutes southwest of Las Vegas and off what is now Interstate 15. *Étude pour une fin du monde n. 2* ("Study for an End of the World, Number 2") was one of the artist's trademark kinetic works assembled from found materials, with its largest component standing over thirty feet tall. Billed as a self-destroying machine, once set into motion at 4:51 P.M. on March 21, it burned and exploded while being filmed. Several smoke bombs and twenty thousand firecrackers sent smoke three hundred feet into the air. The assembled journalists, more of

Jean Tinguely, *Étude pour une fin du monde n. 2* **("Study for an End of the World, Number 2"), Las Vegas, 21 March 1962.** Photos by Coliene Murphy and John Bryson for *Life*. (above) **closeup of control board;** (below) **detonation.**

whom covered this event than anything else that had happened near Las Vegas since the first atomic bomb tests, took shelter behind plywood barricades.

The event was the kind of activity that the artist Allan Kaprow had recently labeled a "happening," and embodied Tinguely's conviction that life was always in flux and transformation. He believed that to attempt its capture in a static artwork was not only futile but senseless, a philosophical stance that would prove relevant to many contemporary artworks in the desert.

Germano Celant, the celebrated art critic, curator, and author of the largest book on Heizer, states that "except for the precedent of Jean Tinguely . . . no artist, before Heizer, had ever explored such areas of silence and emptiness." That's a bit of an overstatement, given the work of the topographical artists in the 1800s and of the photographers and painters earlier in the twentieth century. And Tinguely was just using Jean Dry Lake as one in a series of mock-apocalyptic stages for his post-Dadaist gestures. Playas were still not exactly known to art critics or audiences as either the subject of art or the location of it. Heizer would change all that.

Between January and May of 1968, Heizer used shovels and pickaxes to carve works in the Mojave on Coyote Dry Lake, just north-northeast of Barstow, and on the El Mirage playa outside Victorville. Later that summer, he excavated or reinforced numerous existing negative spaces across 520 miles of the Nevada desert, the individual elements made more or less simultaneously as parts of a single sculpture, *Nine Nevada Depressions*. Angular zigzag lines, curving loops, straight troughs, and intersections were all linked metaphorically across the desert as the world's largest sculpture. *Rift*, the first of *Nevada Depressions*, was made, appropriately enough, on Jean Dry Lake; the final one was *Isolated Mass/Circumflex* made on the bed of Massacre Lake, a sometimes-dry playa that sits northwest of the Black Rock Desert near the conjunction of the Nevada, California, and Oregon borders. Some of the individual elements of the sculpture began to disappear within two weeks of completion; others took longer, but none remain visible today.

Nineteen sixty-eight was the year that marked the official birth of "earthworks" as an art movement, though it's a term that sits uneasily with Heizer. He continued to make sculptures on the playas throughout that year, as well as helping Walter De Maria construct his own *Mile Long Drawing,* two parallel lines of white chalk four inches wide and four yards apart running across a playa. Heizer had met De Maria, like him a Californian but ten years older, in New York in 1966, and convinced him to take a road trip in April out to the desert. De Maria had been designing a series of proposals from 1960 to 1964 that included a huge sculpture in the desert, two parallel walls running alongside each other meant to be walked inside, but he hadn't yet done any work on the land. *Mile Long Drawing* was, in essence, a study for that work.

Heizer wasn't just making sculpture in 1968 but enormous drawings as well, and he also executed his *Black Dye and Powder Dispersal 1* and *2* on Coyote Dry Lake, spreading water-based chromatic pigments out on the playa surface to be scattered by wind—artworks that would dissolve entirely with a few changes of the weather. Early in 1969, Heizer made his *Primitive Dye Paintings,* again on the Coyote playa. Later that year, with a commission from a German art dealer, he was able to afford earthmoving equipment for the first time and promptly returned to that playa to excavate *Triple Landscape* and *Five Conic Displacements.* A telling photograph of the latter taken from the air shows a figure standing next to a piece of equipment parked beside a single-engine airplane. Not only does the earthmover give us the size of the drawing, which has become a sculptural figure incised in the ground, but the airplane allows us to imagine scale: you have to fly over this art in order to grasp it fully.

Nineteen sixty-nine, another incredibly busy year for Heizer, saw him continuing to investigate the possibilities of negative sculpture when he transferred three granite slabs weighing thirty, fifty-two, and sixty-eight tons from Spooner Summit above Lake Tahoe down to holes dug in the flats at Silver Springs. *Displaced/Replaced Mass 1* was the first of three such sculptures made over several years, the apotheosis of which was the construction of *Double Negative*. Heizer purchased sixty acres on the edge of Mormon Mesa, a site above the Virgin River eighty miles northeast of Las Vegas, and began construction that year on the two huge incisions, each fifty feet deep and thirty feet wide that displaced a total of 240,000 tons of material onto debris fans below. The trenches ran downward at forty-five degrees and faced each other across a bowl in the side of the mesa, thereby making a single visual unit 1,800 feet long.

In 1970, Heizer finished *Double Negative* and also executed two large playa drawings. Leasing surface rights from the Bureau of Land Management, he directed motorcycles in a series of circles on Jean Dry Lake. *Circular Surface Planar Displacement Drawing* and *Tangential Drawing* were documented extensively both from the air and from a scaffold erected specifically for that purpose. The twenty-four-foot tower was built on wheels and moved sixteen feet at a time along one of the four-hundred-foot-diameter circles in order to photograph continuously its circumference.

During the same eventful year that he and De Maria drove out to the desert, Heizer met the New Jersey-born Robert Smithson (1938–1973) at New York City's now-legendary Max's Kansas City Bar. They soon made trips together to Connecticut and New Jersey to locate places for Smithson to execute some of his *Site/Nonsite* works. Sampling materials from the landscape, he placed them in neutral boxes and displayed them in galleries and museums with topo maps of their original location, a conceptual counterbalance to Heizer's work. Heizer invited Smithson to visit the desert, which he did that summer of 1968, bringing his partner, Nancy Holt (1938–), with him. Heizer took Smithson to Mono Lake, among other places in California, Nevada, and Utah. While at the lake—a stark Pleistocene relict body of water situated between the steep ramparts of the eastern Sierra and the desert mountains—he collected volcanic cinders and fragments for one of his *Site/Nonsite* pieces and made a short Super-8mm film. In turn, Smithson helped Heizer dig the trenches for at least one of the *Nine Nevada Depressions*.

In October 1969, a show titled "Earthworks," which had been organized by Smithson for the Dwan Gallery and featured work by Heizer, De Maria, and others, opened in New York. The title was lifted from a dystopian science-fiction novel by Brian Aldiss, which had been published in England in 1965 and bought in a 1967 Signet paperback reprint by Smithson, an avid sci-fi reader. That year, Smithson also traveled to the Yucatán, and—clearly in homage to Heizer and his father—placed mirrors on the ground in nine locations and photographed them to create *Nine Mirror Displacements,* again a reversed carbon-copy of Heizer's work.

Although Smithson had made only one earthwork himself by that year—*Asphalt Rundown,* a mass poured into a quarry near Rome, Italy—he was already writing a series of texts that would make him the most prominent theoretician of the artists working in the movement. Shortly after *Double Negative* was completed in 1970, Smithson made *Spiral Jetty* on the edge of the Great Salt Lake. A 1,500-foot-long by 15-foot-wide spiral of black basalt and limestone rocks filled with dirt, the spiral was located at one of the few places on the lake where the water came up to a steep shoreline, thus providing an elevated vantage point from which to view—and photograph—the sculpture. In addition, rusting equipment was scattered around the area and nearby was an abandoned oil-well rig. It was as if Smithson had found a western counterpart to the industrial New Jersey landscape that was his home territory.

Heizer was already at work on his next project, which involved buying up 1,800 acres in a remote valley floor in south-central Nevada, a place where he continues a major effort to make *City,* a series of sculptures inspired by ancient Egyptian and Mesoamerican sources and arrayed inside a mile-long trench. Visible from the air but meant to be experienced while walking the floor of the pit, the enormous berms, beams, walls, stelae, and other forms resonate with each other on a scale so large, yet so well-balanced, that they seem to generate their own peculiar gravity when you're next to them.

Smithson would perish in a plane crash over Texas in 1973, and De Maria would go on to make another signature piece in the movement, the *Lightning Field* in New Mexico, which was started in 1974 and finished in 1977. Other artists would trek from New York and elsewhere to use the playas for their work, including Dennis Oppenheim, who in 1978 poured four lines of asphalt primer and cobalt-blue dry pigment to make two converging two-thousand-foot-long needle shapes on El Mirage Dry Lake, a work titled *Cobalt Vectors—An Invasion*. He also poured out another two lines of the same length on the playa in a giant X, a work titled *Relocated Burial Ground*. The influence of the two gestures, when considered in light of the popular science-fiction television series about aliens, *The X-Files,* which in turn was often shot in the desert, is clear evidence of how desert and media cohabit one another, and a prime example of culture and nature colliding with one another.

Earthworks as a movement, in the meantime, would soon split into two camps, those making long-term installations, such as Heizer and James Turell with his *Roden Crater* project in the northern Arizona desert, and temporary or ephemeral works, such as those by Richard Long, Hamish Fulton, and Andy Goldsworthy. In addition to the philosophical differences underlying the two approaches, money and bureaucracy were increasingly intruding upon art in the American deserts.

By 1976, the BLM was required by law to institute a permitting process to insure the preservation of desert lands. If Tinguely, for example, were still alive and wanted to blow up his sculptures on a playa today, he would need to pay for law enforcement, fire officials, sanitation, and insurance, among other items. The permitting process for artists working on public lands has become so exhaustive that Christo, the artist who runs fences over hill and dale into the ocean and wraps enormous tarps around everything from historical monuments to islands, has expanded his definition of installation art to include documenting the bureaucratic maze as part of his pieces.

The largest art project currently taking place on any playa in the world is the Burning Man Festival, which occurs every Labor Day Weekend in the Black Rock Desert. More than twenty thousand artists and participants pay from $100 to $300 apiece to attend, the millions raised necessary to pay fees to the BLM and to create the temporary civic infrastructure required by officials. Michael Heizer is able to work on his enormous sculptural environment only because he first bought the land, then worked out a legal arrangement with the Dia Center for the Arts in New York to protect it with a nonprofit umbrella. Dia also now maintains De Maria's *Lightning Field* and Smithson's *Spiral Jetty*, both of which would simply disintegrate over time without endowed funds to support them and attorneys skilled in negotiating with government agencies.

Other artists have gone in the opposite direction, minimizing their profile in order to slip beneath the radar of officialdom. Richard Long was displacing the ground beneath his feet to make art interventions in the landscape starting as early as 1964, when he was photographing the tracks of snowballs. While Heizer was carving sculptures into the dry lakes of the Mojave, Long was making paths in English meadows by repeatedly walking across the vegetation and creating a transitory mark. Ever since, he's been recording similar evidence of his travels in a variety of settings around the world. In 1981, he was in Bolivia, both kicking stones into a line and removing them from another line, then photographing these positive and negative versions of his passage, a reference to the Nazca lines. In 1989, he worked in the Anatolian region of Turkey, one of those areas of inward-draining basins that Frémont was referring to when he said that the Great Basin excited our "Asiatic imagination." He visited Big Bend, Texas, in 1990, clearing circles in the desert along the Rio Grande.

Among the works by Long that I personally admire most is a series of 1988 walks made in the Hoggar of the Sahara, one of the great stony deserts that Long favors. When interviewed, the artist has little to say about his aesthetics, relying on his intuition to respond to local conditions. He had started cutting and moving turf around in his parents' backyard when much younger, and he still relies most on how the ground feels in his hands and under his feet to guide his actions. The Sahara work includes circles of cleared and/or stacked stones, straight lines, and meandering paths, as well as performance pieces such as *Two Sahara Stones:*

SITTING ON A MOUNTAINTOP

IN THE HOGGAR

CLAPPING TWO FLAT STONES TOGETHER

A THOUSAND TIMES

1988

Long and that other great English artwalker, Hamish Fulton, along with their younger and quite renowned colleague Andy Goldsworthy, don't work much on playas per se but commit modest and usually temporary interventions on barren tracts of land, their photographs of which then become traces of their passage (as in Long), their diaries (Fulton), or the objects shown in galleries (Goldsworthy). These artworks, which are part performance and part site-specific installation, are acts of cognitive participation that constantly remind us of how we have, through our actions, transformed land into landscape for millions of years. The arid and frozen places of the world are ideal for these activities, because even our most subtle gestures are visible there.

The issues of time in the desert and the mortality of art are crucial to understanding art on the playas—"on" as in meaning both "about" and "sited upon." The Great Basin isn't a particularly ancient landscape, but time is remarkably visible within it, as in most deserts, because of the lack of vegetation. It's not just our sense of space that both disorients us in deserts and influences the artworks found there, but also time.

The earth formed about 4.6 billion years ago; the oldest rocks visible in the region are pre-Paleozoic metamorphic rocks in northwestern Utah, up near the Idaho-Nevada border, and are schists 2.5 billion years old. But the southern portion of what we know as the contemporary Great Basin wasn't even part of the North American continent until 1.74 billion years ago. Fossil algae, trilobites, and echinoderms show us that 600 million years ago, during the Paleozoic, the western part of the basin was under deep water, eastern Utah and Las Vegas were sitting under a shallow sea, and in between, what is now western Utah and eastern Nevada was a continental shelf. To give you an idea of where we are in the timeline, remember that North America didn't separate from Eurasia until 80 million years ago, which was when the continental plates under what would be the Pacific Ocean first began to deform the western United States, though the exact how and why of this will keep geologists employed for decades to come.

Readers interested in the full history of the region's formation should take a look at Bill Fiero's well-illustrated *Geology of the Great Basin*, but to make an interesting long story unmercifully short, although the constituent materials of Nevada and Utah are reasonably old, the basin-and-range topography of the region didn't start to form until 17 million years ago. The crust of the earth was stretched and uplifted in an immense dome over an area a thousand miles long and three to six hundred miles wide between the Sierra Nevada and the Wasatch Mountains, in places distending the crust by as much as 100 percent. What was at the time a relatively featureless volcanic plain was cracked as it rose, forming the rising flanks of what would become more than three hundred mountain ranges in Nevada alone; large blocks dropped down in between the uplifted ranges, doing so with some uniformity. The Great Basin would hold within its boundaries more than a hundred separately enclosed sub-basins, many of which would come to hold playas when the glaciers that grew in the mountains 3 million years ago finally retreated to roughly their current limits as late as 13,000 years before the present.

The point is that, even though the playas are so young as to be invisible on the timeline of the mountains and rocks surrounding them, because all this complicated and folded geology is exposed as sequential stratigraphy in the desert, we are immersed in what since the seventeenth century we understand as visible time. Making something with the arrogance to presume permanence in the face of such patently deep time is ludicrous, as Jean Tinguely well understood. If the twentieth century has left us with anything, it's an understanding grounded in mathematics, physics, and chemistry that the world is more about process than product. Anyone who lives in the earthquake-prone Great Basin can testify to this. It's a place still in the making.

Then there's the matter of art itself, nearly 100 percent of which in some cultures has disappeared within only a few centuries of its creation. Fire, flood, and earthquakes . . . insects, internal decay, and smog . . . and those are just the natural causes. In the category of culturally impelled causalities, there are war, divorce, and ritual burial with the deceased, not to mention de-accession through the trash. Curators, archivists, and librarians routinely, albeit with regret, de-accession up to 90 percent of their holdings in order to preserve what they consider at the time to be the remaining most valuable 10 percent. The most successfully preserved art in the history of the world, that of the ancient Egyptians, which was placed in tombs and sealed away, has been plundered in grave robberies of up to 99 percent of known burials. And those objects excavated since 1800, as art historian Gary Schwartz points out in his 1996 article, "Ars Moriendi: The Mortality of Art," have simply resumed their place in the flow of entropy. Even rocks rot, as Fiero points out. How could we think that art would last?

Art history, however, has built an elaborate academic edifice on the assumption that what is preserved is the best and most important. Heizer and his earthmoving contemporaries, in deliberately leaving the gallery scene of New York City and its preemptive purchasing of material culture, were attempting to create an art outside of a predatory flow of goods that moved up a food chain from artist to gallery to patron to museum. Earthworks ended up being owned, of course, capitalism having its own persistencies. *Double Negative* sat at first on land purchased for the artist by his dealer, Virginia Dwan, and now resides *in situ* for the collection of the Museum of Contemporary Art in Los Angeles, which is allowing the sculpture, one of the most-visited earthworks in the world, its mortality. It's a magnificent monument to entropy as it slowly erodes, and although Heizer now admits that he would like to repurchase it, clean up its edges, stabilize the walls with a mixture of cement and native material, and arrest the decay, the idea that most of his desert works are ephemeral is one that still appeals to many in the art world.

The freeway that Matt Coolidge and I are following on our way to witness the entropy at *Double Negative* splits at Barstow, with I-40 veering east to Needles and Phoenix and I-15 continuing northeast to Las Vegas. We take the latter, and the first playa of the trip appears ahead of us, a small unnamed flat underneath the Calico Mountains. On the far side of the varicolored hills and invisible from the freeway sits Coyote Dry Lake. As if Coyote's history with Heizer weren't enough, Matt says he's been contacted by a gentleman who says that the playa is now used in the power grid as a giant resistor, the "Coyote Dry Lake Return Electrode." The idea is that power is dumped into the ground, modified, sucked back out. Could be true, could be a rumor—Matt hopes to have time someday to track it down for possible addition to the CLUI database.

Coolidge is, however, already a rolling call-out of the military and industrial installations that we're passing, and he's rattling off what's stored out on the Mojave Airport (Delta's old L10–11 passenger jets and the front half of a 747 that served as Harrison Ford's *Air Force One* in the eponymously titled film, among other things). He points out where a giant hydraulic lift raises an entire jet out of the ground for covert radar scans of Stealth technology, then quickly lowers it in order to avoid being photographed by hostile satellites. Following the topo map displayed on the laptop, an hour later he drives us up to the top of Turquoise Peak east of Baker for a look at what was once a Cold War strategic communications site. Now its multiple towers and reinforced concrete structure built three stories deep into the mountaintop are leased by AirTouch Cellular and other corporations. Two helicopters *whup-whup* off to the north, and he identifies them as Apache attack models.

Arrayed out along the horizon are the Kelso Dunes to the south and the Dumonts to the northwest, and Silver and Soda Dry Lakes that bracket Baker. All along our route now there will be salt and alkali flats, next being the Ivanpah and Roach Dry Lake playas at the California and Nevada state line, which display vividly the changing relationships among the playas, the military, and the arts. The military doesn't drop as many bombs on the desert as it used to, instead using simulators more and more to mimic the accuracy of pilots acquiring ground targets.

Phil Patton examines the shift in his book *Dreamland*, in which he analyzes that paragon playa of military development, Area 51, or Groom Lake, as it's more commonly called by its users. He notes that the entertainment industry has replaced the armed forces as leaders in the development of simulators, the youth audience for video games having driven mass-media corporations to supplant the military as the primary technological innovator. In a related development, we're slowly moving the overall use of the desert from the military bases of World War II to the commercial sector in the twenty-first century, a shift in society that will show up vividly on the Ivanpah playa, where Las Vegas will construct a new airport. The Ivanpah playa is the only spot within a thirty-five-mile radius of Las Vegas that can hold the required 6,500-acre site. At first handling only cargo, then international traffic, the airport is projected to open within the decade, despite the protests of environmentalists seeking to protect the viewshed of the Mojave National Preserve.

We don't stop to examine the huge twin playas at the state border, but head for a detour to Jean Dry Lake before entering Las Vegas. A few miles past the state line, we pull off at the entrance to the hamlet of Jean, pass over a short rise among low hills, and drive out onto the surprisingly intimate space of the playa.

It's easy to see why Tinguely, Heizer, and others would have chosen to work here. It's close to the road but visually isolated from it, a blank page large enough to drive on, yet one with a border of sagebrush within a few hundred yards to define the space, qualities that also make it popular with media producers. One of the more recent shoots conducted here was a re-creation of the classic Mint 400 off-road race for the movie *Fear and Loathing in Las Vegas,* a sporting event that gonzo journalist Hunter S. Thompson was sent to Las Vegas to cover, and the original reason for the trip that he immortalized in his book of the same name.

Today, an auto-transport truck and several location vans are parked out near the playa's center, a film crew from California wiping down several red Chevys in preparation for an advertising shoot. We circle them once, wave, then park near a large berm to take notes. Within less than a minute, a small truck peels away from the crew and pulls up alongside us. An unshaven man wearing a stained cowboy hat leans unsteadily out of the driver's window. A younger and much larger specimen lurks in the passenger seat.

"What're you doin' here?"

"Taking notes about the desert. Looks like that's a film crew over there from California," I reply, hoping for some information.

"Think so?" The guy's tone is belligerent, not to mention heavy with slurred consonants, so I climb back in the van. He circles us in short bursts, popping his clutch like a teenager looking for a fight, and eying the CLUI logo with obvious suspicion. Matt puts the van in gear, and we cruise west a couple of hundred yards, hoping to be left in peace.

No such luck. After its driver consults with someone in one of the other vehicles, the truck follows, then pulls in front of us. We're right in the middle of comparing a photograph of Heizer's *Rift* with the profile of the surrounding hills, hoping to pin down its location. This time the cowboy gets out.

"Shut 'er down," he commands, making a sloppy twisting motion with his hand. Matt and I don't even bother to look at each other, knowing we'll do no such thing, the start to every bad slice-and-dice movie set in the desert we've ever seen. Matt keeps the engine on and repositions the van slightly so we have a free exit.

"Mister, I don't have a problem with you, so what's your problem with us?"

"I don' know who you are, tha's my problem."

Matt points down at the logo on the door, explains we're a non-profit organization, and then adds that we're not with the government, just for insurance.

The old guy glares at us, holds up a cell phone, and declares, "I'm a federal marshal. I'm gonna call you in." He staggers back to his truck and we simply leave, not knowing if he's been hired by the film crew to keep the slate of the playa wiped clean for their shoot, or is just another whacked-out Sagebrush Rebellion goon drunk with anger over public ownership of the land. In either case, it's not exactly how we'd hoped to begin our trip.

Three hours later, it's a completely different story. We've continued east and north to Overton, an agricultural town on the back reaches of Lake Mead, and the jumping-off point for people visiting *Double Negative*. Word is that the road up the Mormon Mesa escarpment has been ground into deep dust at its steepest point and is passable only in a four-wheel drive. Matt has come prepared, though, with the name of a local pilot who will fly us up for a look at the Heizer sculpture and a quick search for a nearby De Maria work, *Las Vegas Piece,* a rectangle of lines drawn in the desert floor.

Dallas Nichols, a former Alaskan bush pilot, meets us just before 6 P.M., gasses up his Piper Cherokee, and takes us up for a spin over the mesa. Nichols is tan and cheerfully middle aged, wearing jeans and a polo shirt.

"Yeah, I've flown people from all over the world up here, maybe fifty trips to see *Double Negative* in the nine years I've been doin' it. Some people cry when they see it, this German guy, he went up twice, cried both times.

"It's really crumblin', I think that upsets some people. You'll see. We'll orbit around it a couple different ways, and you can see how it's deteriorating."

He banks the plane east, circles over the road so we can see how it's been chewed into dust, then heads east again toward the Virgin River side of the mesa. From takeoff to *Double Negative* is all of eight minutes in the air, the long cuts in the sides of the embayment soon visible, long shadows cast deeply into the earth by late afternoon sun.

I've never been here before, though have written about the sculpture from photographs, and am surprised at the emotion it evokes. The front edge of the west, or mesa side, of the north cut in particular is caving in, as is to a lesser degree the outer east edge of the south cut, but I don't find that too disturbing. Then, too, the fans of displaced material below the cuts, which are also part of the sculpture, have begun to blur as vegetation reestablishes itself. The decay of man-made forms in the desert is the rule, not the exception. What moves me is the space itself.

Dallas keeps saying it's "just a hole in the ground," but he's also read enough to know it means more, and actually quotes Heizer from memory about the meaning of, the physical impossibility of, two negatives. He gets it—that the empty space in between the two excavations multiplies the amount of displaced mass, that it's a sculpture about what's not there.

And that's what it is. All the art history aside, when Dallas takes a low pass over the mesa and drops us abruptly below the lip, so that we're actually staring into the open maw of the cuts, we're in the presence of a void so large that it's architectonic, two spaces that resonate unexpectedly across a natural void. It's like being in a temple for a fleeting moment. If we were standing inside the ground on the floor of one of the cuts, presumably we'd get something of the feeling, but being suspended in midair between the two is a combinatory moment. Everything you know and don't about the sculpture comes together. It's visceral, a sensation aided and abetted by the sudden absence of ground beneath us as the plane drops off the mesa. And it's also a feeling you can't maintain, since you're already moving away from it when it occurs. As we bank left and upriver, I realize that it's a classic case of indeterminacy. You can only get this knowledge of where *Double Negative* resides by being in motion, thus you can't pin down the experience at your leisure. No doubt Werner Heisenberg would have approved.

Dallas takes us up north to look for the De Maria piece, which he's tried to locate before at the behest of curators and critics. "I've flown grids up here for years tryin' to find this thing." Mile-long lines carved eight feet wide into the desert scrub in the late 1960s should still be visible, we think, given that Patton's tank tracks are famously still discernible. But as we quarter the valleys north of Mormon Mesa at three thousand feet above the ground for an hour, we begin to agree with Dallas.

"Listen, all those roads and trails down there?"—the floor of every valley is crossed and recrossed by multiple dirt tracks—"Maybe a rancher comes through, or some mining company, and they see this road, or what they think is a road, and they just extend it. I mean, when I first saw a photograph of it, I thought it just looked like section lines. And everyone puts their roads on section lines. I think it's just become part of all this other stuff, so you can't see it anymore. Even if it's not overgrown, even if the lines are still there, it's invisible."

The possible absorption of art by one of its progenitors, cartography, has a certain appropriateness to it, and we give up. I've speculated before that the first visual representation made by hominids may have been lines drawn in the dirt to indicate directions to food, and I have no trouble imagining the held-over cartographic imperative of the nineteenth-century West, a process brought here by Frémont and Preuss, reclaiming the ground of the artistic figure.

The sun has already set by the time we fly back into Overton, passing one end of the Valley of Fire as we do so, the red sandstone still a warm presence in the landscape as if it had absorbed some of the sunlight and was letting it slowly evaporate in the early evening. We could have stayed up for hours longer, Matt and I, just watching the landscape change beneath us. In fact, Matt actually took flying lessons, but he quit just before getting his pilot's license when he realized it wasn't the flying he cared about, but examining what was below him.

Driving back to Las Vegas in the dark, Matt explains what he's looking for in the earthworks, evidence for the premise of a CLUI exhibition that he's curating on how time has affected the artworks, which will be titled "Formations of Erasure: Earthworks and Entropy."

"What I'm interested in is how nature first shapes the land, then how man changes it as a geomorphological agent. And then, how nature comes back in and co-sculpts results that weren't necessarily anticipated."

This is a cycle of activity that is more apparent in the desert, of course, than elsewhere, given the lack of vegetation. And nowhere else will that process be more starkly visible than during the next two days, when we go to visit the Department of Energy's Las Vegas office, and then the Nevada Test Site.

A Tour of the Playa   Part II: The Nevada Test Site

The Department of Energy's North Las Vegas Facility on Losee Road doesn't look like much from outside the fence. There's the mothballed fourteen-story "high bay" tower at one corner, where they used to assemble the instrument packages that would hold the nuclear devices in place for the detonations, but it's a bland structure that doesn't look as large as it really is unless examined closely. There are office buildings with a variety of official signs and guard posts, but it's not until you enter the property and meet the gentlemen from Wackenhut that you begin to appreciate the difference between this and, say, a university research park or a chemical plant.

My image of security guards is based on the ex-cops who prowl the carpeted floors of casinos. The relationship between those civilian security people and the DOE contractors is, as I discover, that of Labrador puppies to grown Rottweilers. The Wackenhut guys, many of them former Navy SEALs and U.S. Army Special Forces personnel, are dressed in desert camo fatigues and carry formidable sidearms. Some installations on the Test Site are routinely subjected to serious raids by active Special Forces units tasked to capture them—and Wackenhut defends them successfully. Just speaking to these guys in a booth by the parking lot makes me nervous, a feeling that only gets worse when it turns out they're not expecting us until the next afternoon, when we're scheduled to show up for a briefing.

It turns out to be a small though complicated snafu. The briefing is actually for Jonathan Veitch, a writer from New York who's going with us to do an article on the Test Site for *Harper's* magazine. His plane has been rerouted to Phoenix because of weather, and he won't get here until this evening. Plus, the woman scheduled to do the briefing is out with a thrown back. It's a testament to Matt's standing at the Test Site that they don't tell us to go away; instead, they pull in Jeff Gordon, a public-relations guy from the major contractor at the site, Bechtel Nevada, to handle us. The CLUI *Guide to the Nevada Test Site* is a publication valued by the DOE because it saves them time and effort, showing people what's out there without any proselytizing. I get the feeling that the CLUI makes them a little wary but that they figure it's better to go along than not.

Visitation to the Test Site is down to forty to eighty people per month, most of the traffic now going to Yucca Mountain, the controversial nuclear-waste storage site proposed to start accepting high-level radioactive materials possibly as soon as 2005. The NTS staff is down from 12,000 to around 2,300 people since the 1992 moratorium on testing was passed, with 300 of those DOE and other federal employees. The rest are Bechtel and Wackenhut personnel, and a few other associated contractors. Apart from its ongoing "stewardship" of the nation's nuclear stockpile—which means the testing, maintenance, and occasional upgrading of existing warheads—what the DOE is attempting to do is convert the NTS mission into one of commercial usage. Jeff, speaking over the phone with someone to arrange passage for us into the visitor's center, actually reminds them that, after all, "We're into customer service here."

Despite the fact that Matt and I are intrigued by the conflation of a term we normally associate with the conservation of nature, *stewardship,* with the handling of bombs, and that Jeff has to get a security authorization to unlock a "visitor's" center, we're cognizant of how the NTS has opened up increasingly over the years. We watch a twenty-minute videotape of excerpts from the twelve most-recent additions to the ninety declassified government films now available to the public that depict nuclear-bomb tests and Broken Arrow incidents. It's with some amazement that I witness recovery crews combing wreckage in Spain, Greenland, and Yuba City, California, for parts from bombs accidentally dropped and/or lost in bomber crashes. When we finally get into the visitor's center, we find photographs of everything on the Test Site from petroglyphs to blurbs for "VentureStar," a private aerospace company hoping to launch the next-generation space shuttle, an operation that the NTS is attempting to lure onto the property. A gift shop, which is closed, offers T-shirts, hats, and mugs.

Photos on the walls also show how nuclear waste is being stored in subsidence craters created by underground tests, and how old buildings are now used to train first responders, mainly firefighters and police, to everything from hazardous-materials spills to terrorism with weapons of mass destruction.

"So, you have a policy of reusing existing facilities?" I ask.

"Not really," is the response. "It's on a case-by-case basis."

I ponder this, knowing that governments in general, and the military in particular, prefer overall policies and guidelines to having to make individual decisions. Looking around at the artifacts donated by old-timers who worked at the site, as well as drawings by local architects for the extensive Nevada Atomic Testing History Institute, which will be built on the University of Nevada, Las Vegas campus next year, I have another question.

"Is there nostalgia for the old days at the Site?"

"No, not at all," replies Jeff. "We can't even get volunteers in here on a regular basis to keep the place open. People are happy to be working elsewhere. They're making more money." For a moment he seems to lose his professional composure and actually looks glum, perhaps contemplating his own position, but I also know that people don't give away mementos from world-class engineering projects, versus saving them for their kids, without sentimental reasons for doing so.

Jeff and others give us a full two hours of their time, and we walk out with stacks of press releases and other materials that public-relations people refer to as "collaterals." I wonder if the almost-automatic denial by NTS people to all questions is part of the DOE culture, or simply PR-speak. Maybe the two are more closely related than I had assumed. It's also tempting to wonder if the 350,000 documents about the Site that have been declassified under the Clinton Administration (and the 300,000 more they haven't the budget to scan) are one enormous blizzard of paper obscuring what it is that remains secret.

Matt and I reflect upon this in the car, and he repeats a statement that's becoming more and more of a refrain with writers and photographers who document how humans use land.

Robert Cole Caples. *Red Mountain.* **Ca. 1941. Pastel on paper, 18 x 24 inches.** Collection of the Nevada Museum of Art, The Samuel G. Houghton Collection of Great Basin Art

Stuart D. Klipper. *Road to Bonneville Raceway, Utah.* **1990. From the series** *The World in a Few States.* Reproduced with the permission of Stuart D. Klipper

Richard Misrach, *Ammunition Storage Bunkers, Wendover Air Base, Utah.* 1990. Reproduced with the permission of Richard Misrach

Richard Misrach, *Downed Safety Cone, Bonneville Salt Flats, Utah.* **1992.** Reproduced with the permission of Richard Misrach

Craig Sheppard. *Black Rock Desert*. **Photograph by Dean Burton.** Reproduced with the permission of John Lewis

Michael Moore. *Black Rock Desert, October 6.* **1996–97. Acrylic on canvas, 60 x 60 inches.**
Photograph ©1997 by Jacques Cressaty. Reproduced with the permission of Michael Moore

Mike Woolson. *The Temple of the Mind by David Best.* (above) *Before;* (below) *After.* Copyright 2000. All rights reserved.

"I want to make the world a more interesting place so people will pay attention to it. People stop paying attention to what you're saying if they think everyone is telling them what to think, trying to convince them of something. They get reductive and turn off seeing things."

"You mean to not be ironic all the time about what we're seeing?"

Matt nods. "It's important to have alternative views of the world. That's what CLUI provides, I hope—an alternative view outside academia." Matt doesn't propose that there are or aren't secrets hidden at the Test Site, nor is he interested in applying literary deconstructionism to the language of the DOE. He'd prefer to let the audience view the documentation that the CLUI presents and make up its own mind.

Seven a.m. the next morning, we're back in the DOE parking lot next to a white Pontiac containing what turns out to be a very tall, genial, and somewhat apologetic Jonathan Veitch. A professor in the humanities department at New York's New School, he's writing a book about how certain places in America that once loomed large in the public imagination have fallen out of that realm, places such as Niagara Falls, Pittsburgh, and the Test Site.

Within a few minutes, we're joined by Derek Scammel, who drives up in the white Jeep Cherokee that we'll use for our tour. Almost every car in the rapidly filling parking lot is white, the color of choice in a climate where temperatures can exceed 120° Fahrenheit.

Scammel has become well known as a guide to the Test Site, where he's been schlepping media people around for twelve years. Born in East London but having served his entire adult life in service to the American government, first in the military and now with the DOE, his English accent remains intact, accompanied by an affable yet nononsense demeanor that presumably won't show the slightest slippage all day long.

After minor preliminaries, we load ourselves into the Jeep and drive north toward Mercury, the town that serves as the major entry point for the Test Site. We have a minute-by-minute itinerary of the locations Matt and Jonathan have requested to visit, which projects us finishing around nine tonight, but Scammel thinks we'll be able to accomplish everything by sunset. At one point he questions whether Matt really wants to go clear out to the Buckboard Mesa area, which is seldom visited by outsiders, and Matt replies that it's necessary to verify information for the new edition of the guidebook. The Test Site, an area about the size of Rhode Island, resides entirely within the Nellis Air Force Range, an additional 4,120 square miles that make it larger than Connecticut and almost the size of Israel. (Nevada, the seventh largest state in the Union, could cram all of New England and Hawaii within its borders and still have room left over for the Test Site, a fact in which its residents take pride, hence the oft-repeated comparisons with members of the original colonies.)

Derek has a standard spiel for visitors but gets only part way into it before Matt begins to query him on the status of certain valleys, such as the infamous Area 51, which he's heard has been ceded by the DOE to the air force in a trade for a small extension of the Test Site into the Nellis Range. The exchange reputedly was made in order to capture some ground contaminated by the 1968 Schooner shot, a shallow underground test that sent fallout as far away as Montreal.

"Groom Lake, you mean. Only civilians call it Area 51. Yes, it's air force now." Our trip isn't about probing the intense subculture of UFO-watchers that has fetishized Groom Lake into the supposed experimental locus of alien presence on-planet, but it's a reminder that the dry lakes of the Great Basin continue to flourish in the American imagination, fueled by media images, even as the traditional scenic climax of a place such as Niagara Falls diminishes.

Jonathan begins to probe politely but insistently about radioactivity, and Scammel sets up his initial lines of defense. First, we won't be exposed to enough radiation to measure during the day, as most radioactivity diminishes relatively quickly over time. Furthermore, radioactivity tends to infect metal and topsoil, most of which has been scooped up and buried. The isolated areas that are still hot we're not allowed into. Matt adds that he's traveled across parts of the Site with a person carrying a Geiger counter, including onto multiple grounds-zero of bomb tests, and the only thing they encountered all day that was radioactive was an orange Fiesta dinner plate in a display case, a ceramic brand notorious for containing traces of uranium.

"Is the future of the Test Site threatened?" Jonathan wants to know.

"Not at all," replies Derek. "There are 42 square miles of contaminated area on the Test Site, and 106 square miles disturbed by the test program—out of a total of 1,375 at the Site. It's clean compared to other DOE sites, such as Rocky Flats in Colorado and Hanford in Washington. Plus, we're looking into establishing a high-tech corridor along the highway parallel to the west side of the Site."

Fifty minutes out of Las Vegas, we pass a relatively small playa to the east and on the Nellis Range. Matt explains it's used for live-fire demonstrations several times a year.

"VIPS are brought in to see how the military is spending its money, and aircraft fly in from all over the country, including B-1 bombers from South Dakota, all choreographed to arrive within a forty-five-minute period to drop bombs in time to rock 'n roll music. People sit in bleachers and watch; there's even a Jumbotron© TV screen so they can catch instant replays. The computer-game company people are really anxious to come see this stuff."

Maybe up close the playa would bear scars from this high-explosive exhibitionism, but from the road it looks level and pristine, just another screen for the media upon which entertainments are projected. Exploitation of the desert for rehearsals in the theater of war never really ceases, despite the increase in private-sector use, and just as the demolition of old high-rise hotels in Las Vegas is filmed by movie studios for later use in action films, so the video-gamers would love to insert footage of the explosions into their more interactive simulations. From this perspective, it's a short arc in aesthetics from Tinguely's exploding sculptures to Stealth-bomber replays at the video arcade.

(above) **Live-fire demonstration on dry lake of Range 63, Nellis Range Complex, showing Jumbotron© screen with live feed.** (below) **Audience for live-fire demonstration.** Both images courtesy CLUI Archive

At 8:10 A.M. we pass the Indian Springs Auxiliary Air Field, a small air force base next to the highway, and Matt continues his rolling commentary. "Look at the hangers at the north end as we pass them. This is where they deploy UAVs, the unmanned aerial vehicles that they used in Kosovo. Usually they're painted white." We don't spot any today, but I've seen pictures of the $25-million Global Hawk, a near relative of the models here. It's a cockpitless craft that looks like a blind albino bat, but it can fly for up to thirty-five hours and as high as 65,000 feet. Made by Northrop Grumman in San Diego and based at Edwards, it may be used mostly for intelligence gathering. The unmanned vehicles still have an unfortunate tendency to veer out of control, however, and the desert remains the safest place to test them.

The synergy of all this — the electronic-game techies filming the military explosions in the Mojave for action backdrops on video screens, games that will be played by a generation of kids who will grow up to control the computer joysticks for unmanned vehicles bombing real targets in, say, a Middle Eastern desert—is more than a little disturbing. The desert, by virtue of disassociating us from a familiar environment, allows us the cognitive room to fantasize more freely. The UFOs of Groom Lake aren't the only results; so are war games.

Just before taking the Mercury exit off the highway, we pass a couple of white vans parked on the opposite shoulder, demonstrators who are engaged in their own kind of intelligence gathering for an Easter assault on the Test Site perimeter. It's not planned to be a very large event, but it is a reminder that we're about to enter a zone that remains hot in terms of politics as well as physics. One group comes to get off on the fireworks; the other wants to see them banned.

Turning off the highway and onto the Test Site, our first stop is at the Wackenhut office, where we check in to receive temporary passes that we clip onto our shirtfronts. We show the passes to the guard at the gate as we drive through; he is required to physically touch each one, an exercise that not only helps ensure his alertness but prevents counterfeiting. Except for two guys driving a fuel truck later in the day, he's the last person we'll see while we cover more than two hundred miles of dirt roads through hundreds of thousands of acres filled with sagebrush, dessicated mountains, and scattered playas. Mercury itself is a proverbial ghost town; its bowling alley, movie house, cafeteria, and gas station—where Derek fills the tank from a pump labeled "No Brand Gasoline"—are all intact but completely empty of people. The place feels like a town emptied by an apocalypse, more an impression generated by watching late-night science-fiction movies than by any connection between radioactivity and the demise of people.

The absence of personnel is partly owing to the severe reductions in staffing after the moratorium, and partly because it's Friday. People work from seven in the morning until five in the evening, and the commutes can run up to two hours each way from Las Vegas, because no one lives on the base—a safety and security precaution. Therefore, Test Site workers pull a four-day week, and Derek is working on what should be his day off, a convenient time to show visitors around while the area is devoid of activity. The abandonment we witness is also, however, compelling evidence of how the status of the Test Site has changed, and why the DOE is so anxious to find commercial uses for it.

Our route today will take us first to the Buckboard Mesa area in the west-northwest quadrant, then gradually work back to the south and into the typical grand tour that Jonathan has requested, but it will also include some rarities for Matt's research. We start by trying to locate one of his priorities, the ground-zero of the Little Feller I explosion, the last of the above-ground nuclear tests, which was conducted in 1962. Taking the Pahute Mesa Road, then turning off on a succession of increasingly less-maintained dirt tracks, Derek has trouble pinpointing the location of the test, as it's been eight to ten years since he was last in this corner of the Site.

Matt spots a tank sitting on a ridge nearby. Because it's painted a faded yellow, at first Derek thinks it's a construction vehicle, but then he sees the turret, its gun barrel drooping toward the ground. We park as close as we can and walk up to a modest wire fence surrounding the small knoll. Derek stays with the Jeep, and I wonder if he's out here so much that he tends to limit his exposure. We're above six thousand feet, the air enough thinner and drier than at sea level to noticeably increase its clarity; the valley we're in looks smaller than it really is, and it's only when peering back down at the Jeep that scale reasserts itself in the mind. It's a joy to be walking around in the high desert again, despite our subject matter.

As we troop around the exclosure, we can't help but step on black cables of varying thickness, all leading inward to ground-zero. Typically, several miles of cable, over a million dollars worth, were used during each test. What makes it possible to measure the effects of a blast is the fact that whereas radiation and electricity travel at the speed of light, the heat and pressure wave travel much slower, enabling signals from test instruments located at ground-zero to outrun the vaporization front of the blast by about a foot.

I kick at the half-buried casing from a 20-caliber cannon round. It's larger than my thumb and a tempting souvenir, but the prohibition against collecting artifacts is not only sound historical preservation, out here it's a commonsense health measure, given radiation's affinity for metal.

Little Feller was a very low-yield device, an atomic bomb fired from a recoilless rifle mounted on an armored personnel carrier. In pictures, the shell itself looks like the cartoon of a bomb, a stubby teardrop the size of a rural mailbox with fins. Lobbed at the site, it exploded about forty feet over the tank in what's known as a "military effects test," an experiment to see what the blast and radiation would do to equipment—in this case, an M48 tank from the 1950s—and its theoretical crew. The tank, while definitely askew and put out of function, is surprisingly intact.

Here's the thing about the fence, however: its perimeter has been moved. The original exclosure, which is still visible, surrounded only a few hundred square yards, but, as Derek has pointed out, rain and wind move the soil around, plus the effects of radiation are better understood all the time. The more-recent boundary includes ten times as much territory. This is not comforting. Not that the cases are exactly comparable, but the nuclear disaster at the Chernobyl power plant in 1986 initially killed thirty-one people, and Soviet authorities predicted that only a few thousand more might be affected by the contamination. As of spring 2000, the Ukraine Health Ministry has declared that 3.5 million people have fallen sick or will be adversely affected as a result of the reactor explosion.

It's not that people lie so much as that bureaucracies tend to remain collectively optimistic in the face of disasters, whether they're tornadoes in Los Angeles or clouds of radioactive fallout. This is because their role is to protect vested interests, whether of capital gains or political power. Bureaucrats are accustomed to downplaying threats to those interests—hence, the calculated verbal habits of the public-relations people the previous day. Status quo is conserved through denial, so it takes a while for the fences to get moved farther out, whether it's at this scale, or expanding the boundary of the Test Site itself to enclose some ground that remains inexplicably hot and on the move.

The fence posts a sign that says RADCON–5, which none of us can translate, including Derek, who claims not to know what it means. It seems obvious, though: a middle range of radiation contamination. I find it surprising that we're standing within a hundred feet of a small ground-zero without so much as a dosimeter, or film badge, pinned to our shirts along with our passes, which would have been the case during previous decades. The irony is that, as the effects of radiation are more thoroughly studied over time, we apparently understand that it's both more and less dangerous than thought earlier. We can, for example, tolerate safely roaming through most of the Test Site, which popular imagination once held permanently hazardous—but now we know that radioactive contamination flows much more quickly through groundwater than was once assumed.

We retrace our way out to Yucca Flat, passing by a fence surrounding ground-zero of the Apple II shot and noting that it's posted as RADCON–10, then bear north to the largest man-made crater in America, the site of the Sedan test. Yucca Flat is the most-bombed landscape on earth, the valley where the majority of the 928 nuclear tests carried out at the Site took place, and the reason why the total disturbed acreage is so small. In just one aerial view of the flat, I once counted at least 135 subsidence craters from underground tests, where the below-surface explosions had imploded enough material to leave behind a pockmark on the surface. The density of the testing was so high that the rims of many craters almost touch each other. We're passing them now, some only a few feet across, others dozens of yards across. The Sedan Crater, however—the most popular tourist attraction on the Site—is entirely something else.

Among the proposed peacetime uses of nuclear power was earthmoving for large construction projects, such as a harbor in Alaska and a new ditch across Central America, the "Panatomic Canal." The series of explosions called the Plowshare Program included shallow tests, such as the Schooner shot, and deep ones like Sedan. For the latter, a 104-kiloton device was lowered 635 feet below the ground; its detonation on July 6, 1962, moved 12 million tons of earth in a millisecond. The crater is 1,280 feet wide, 320 feet deep, and hosts a viewing stand on its lip where we stop for several minutes to take pictures.

Vigorous patches of tumbleweed grow on its steep slopes, and cables lead downward, remnants from lowering various test crews, the Apollo 14 astronauts (who practiced maneuvering around in its lunar-like environment), and even a television news team who broadcast live from the bottom of the crater as a publicity stunt. The spectator stand rises above the lip of the crater to provide a better vantage point for photographers, and there's a railed viewpoint on the lip itself.

Sedan is the only feature at the Site that's listed on the National Register of Historic Places. Personally, I wish they'd declare the entire

Yucca Flat. Photo courtesy of United States Department of Energy

Nevada Test Site as historically significant and bring schoolchildren through here on monitored tours. Seeing the sites of the Civil War is important, but this might have a bit more immediate relevance. In fact, the viewpoint reminds me of nothing so much as the carefully selected points of interest provided by the National Park Service at other scenic climaxes, including that greatest tourist hole of all, the Grand Canyon.

Richard Misrach (1949–), perhaps the most-noted contemporary photographer of the American desert, once photographed a series at the illegal Bravo 20 bombing range in north-central Nevada, then proposed that the area be turned into a national park to commemorate the war waged by the American military on the lands of the West. Richard knew it was political polemic more than an idea that would ever be implemented, but he was serious about it, and it's a notion that has applicability here. If people are so entranced by the military sublime that they want to see explosions and their aftermath, nuclear or not, then we should turn the place into a park and charge admission. The NTS could use the money, and educating Las Vegas tourists about the invention of the largest gamble in the history of mankind—that we can survive our ability to destroy all life on the planet—could be a compelling story in the hands of the public-relations office.

Once again back on the road, Derek plunging back and forth on the empty and crumbling asphalt at fifty to sixty miles an hour, we stop by the fence surrounding the atmospheric Smoky test. This is one of those sites that's never been mopped up, the soil contamination too massive for a cost-effective cleanup. To enter it, you have to be escorted by safety personnel and wear protective clothing that immediately becomes low-level nuclear waste that has to be managed in a storage facility. Smoky, a 9,408-pound thermonuclear device yielding 44 kilotons, was blown up on top of a seven-hundred-foot tower in front of a mountain to see how the proximity of a geophysical feature would affect the blast pattern. The mountain behind it is gray, instead of brown like its surroundings, its soil having been blown off clear down to bedrock. The blast headed up and out to where we're standing, hence we can't see ground-zero directly. We're too far away, but not at all unhappy about it.

Our last stop before lunch is Japan Town, three wooden houses built with traditional materials so the effects of radiation on victims in Hiroshima and Nagasaki could be simulated. Handsome structures in various states of collapse, they were exposed to varying levels of radiation from a bare reactor mounted atop a 1,527-foot tower. The BREN (Bare Reactor Experiment Nevada) tower, which has since been relocated to Jackass Flats, was then the tallest man-made structure in the world, and it still holds the record in America west of the Mississippi—erected years before the Stratosphere Hotel-Casino in Las Vegas claimed a related title, "the tallest building west of the Mississippi," a confusion that annoys Derek. The image of the tower looming over these modest homes dragged around on wooden skids is a severe metaphor for the collision of one technology over another, nuclear blast versus paper walls.

When I think about possible future uses for the Test Site, I imagine Japan Town as a radical counterpoint to the bland internationalism of Disney's Epcot Center. Perhaps an interpretative plaque on the BREN tower could also point out that the initial Operation BREN was conducted during the same week as the Tinguely piece was exploded to the south—also the week when the American Medical Association, apparently in a fit of Cold War patriotism, issued a statement telling the public that it had nothing to fear from exposure to radiation.

A few minutes down the road and we're parked for lunch at one of the "typical American homes" built for the Apple II blast. Once an entire mock town sat here: a school, a library, fire and radio stations, even a small utility grid. Unlike the "Doom Town" that was blown away by the Annie test of 1953, the footage of which has been featured in everything from civil-defense films to the movie *Atomic Cafe,* and in the painting series *The Body of a House* by Las Vegas artist Robert Beckmann, several of these structures survived. We take turns prowling through the decaying rooms, knowing that, as at Japan Town, we could stay here for hours deciphering how a house relates to the idea of home, and of shelter from the "elements." Matt's cell phone rings while he's inside, which strikes us as ludicrously domestic. "Honey, it's for you" is the phrase that comes to mind.

While Jonathan and Matt continue to poke around the house, I lean against the car and talk with Derek. He's guarded about some things, candid about others, perhaps following a rule similar to what guides where photography is allowed here. When the activist and writer Rebecca Solnit toured the Site in 1990 (she subsequently wrote *Savage Dreams: A Journey into the Hidden Wars of the American West*), no recording devices were allowed whatsoever. The rule today is that we can photograph whatever we see. It's only what we're not shown, such as the Groom and Papoose Dry Lakes just over the hills east of us, that we can't record, and that Derek won't discuss.

A site available to the public that we won't visit today, although we'll be skirting its edge, is Yucca Mountain. Within the boundaries of the Test Site, it's nonetheless its own administrative entity, and I ask Derek why.

"Well, it's a bit controversial politically. Senators [Richard] Bryan and [Harry] Reid, for instance, couldn't stay in office if they didn't represent to their Nevada voters that they're against bringing radioactive waste to the state. But Bryan worked here, you know, and we're standing on top of 150 million curies of radioactivity that's underneath the soil from the tests. That's far, far more than would ever be stored at Yucca Mountain.

"Our budget is voted on by Bryan and Reid; we need their support. If we were tied to Yucca Mountain, it would make it harder for them to help us. So, even though we're both on the DOE organizational chart, we keep things separate as much as possible. But I don't think the repository will ever open up."

"Because Nevada will turn it down?" I ask.

"No, because the waste has to be shipped across the country, and every single state it would pass through will sue to stop it."

Derek's assessment agrees with current conventional wisdom, according to newspaper reports, because the waste would have to traverse at least forty states to reach Nevada from its various origins around the country. But it might take only a single disaster at a local storage facility to change peoples' minds. As Derek points out, the waste will flow along the "line of least political resistance," and Nevada has neither the population nor enough seniority in its Congressional delegation to prevent the shipments to Yucca Mountain.

After lunch, we begin the second half of our tour. As we drive down toward the southern end of Yucca Flat, Jonathan asks if the Test Site is in the Mojave or the Great Basin desert. That's a hard question to answer. There are three enclosed basins within the Site: Yucca Flat, which we're just leaving; Frenchman Flat, which we're headed into; and Jackass Flat, which will be our final area of investigation for the day. This puts us, geomorphologically, in Great Basin topology. On the other hand, the Joshua trees we're passing, which are actually the largest members of the lily family, are found only in the Mojave biota.

Two of the flats, Yucca and Frenchman, host dry lakes at their lower southern ends, low points where water runs off the mountains and collects, unable to flow elsewhere on the surface. The visible hydrology, therefore, is Great Basin; yet the playa water here seeps downward into an aquifer underneath us where groundwater flows into the Colorado River Basin. I'm not sure my explanation answers Jonathan's question, a common problem in arid environments where things are never as simple as they look, part and parcel of the cognitive dissonance we suffer in them.

Yucca Lake, as we drive by, appears untouched compared to the majority of Yucca Flat with its hundreds of subsidence craters. Although inert dummies were dropped onto the playa to test the durability of bomb casings, their impacts recorded by high-speed movie cameras, none of the valley's eighty-six above-ground or four hundred underground blasts cratered its surface. Down by its far end stands a rocky outcrop known as News Nob, at the base of which are the sagging wooden bleachers where correspondents sat to watch fourteen atmospheric tests from 1951 through 1962. We pull off the road, Derek once again waiting by the Jeep while we scramble up the rocks to take pictures. From where we stand to where the bombs were detonated—from where Walter Cronkite was made speechless for the only time in his life to those mushroom clouds we've all seen pictures of—was only about three miles. Less than sixteen thousand feet. It seems a preposterously small distance.

It was from here that the first atomic explosion was broadcast on live television in the 1950s, and all I can imagine is that the view across the playa to ground-zero must have scared the shit out of the cameramen. Think of a blast so bright that you could see the bones in your forearms crossed over your closed eyes, as if you were Lot attempting to blot out the destruction of Sodom and Gomorrah. Envision a hot thundercloud boiling up so high over you that you would have to crane back your head as far as it would go to see it. Think of the shock wave passing through you on its way to Las Vegas, only twenty-two seconds away. Think of playas and pillars of salt.

Derek beeps his horn at us politely as we're returning to the Jeep, anxious to keep moving. From our tour of what were the earliest uses of the Test Site we move onto the latest, the storage of low-level nuclear waste. Yucca Mountain, should it open, will accept only high-level radioactive waste, the stuff so hot that it slowly cooks then fractures the very rocks in which it is entombed, and completely resists all human efforts to more than briefly contain it. But then there's all the low-level stuff, such as the protective clothing worn by visitors to the Smoky site, and the mid-level contamination of equipment used in subcritical bomb tests, which are all that are allowed under current international treaties. Not as dangerous as the spent fuel rods that Yucca Mountain might have to accept, these are still byproducts of the military-industrial complex that have to be stored and monitored under controlled circumstances. The low-level pits that we visit in the next valley south, Frenchman Flat, are state-of-the-art: a broad excavation in which waste is stored in drums and boxes, stacked eight to nine deep, then buried. That simple.

Each container is bar-coded and placed within a numbered grid so that specific items can be retrieved, should it be necessary; the simplicity of the arrangement derives from a clear logic: better to know where trouble lies than not. And better to be able to get at it without too much trouble than not. The difference between how this waste is being handled with what's proposed at Yucca Mountain points up a heated argument within the scientific community as well. Entomb the high-level waste so it can spread only minimally, and with a low chance that it will be dispersed more widely by a natural catastrophe, such as an earthquake or volcanic disruption during the tens of thousand of years its radioactivity will remain lethal. Or keep it on or near the surface so that, should new disposal technologies arise, scientists can get at it easily.

Both schemes have another downside. No human language has ever stayed in currency for more than two or three thousand years, and usually for only a few hundred. English is the most ubiquitous language in the world, with seven out of every ten people on the planet using it as their primary or secondary tongue. But all languages change radically over time—imagine if hazard signs were posted in the Middle English of *The Canterbury Tales,* written by Chaucer during the 1390s: the warnings would be incomprehensible to anyone not a professor of English literature.

Artists and others have been hired by the DOE to design prototypes for a "landscape of repulsion" in Project Marker, seeking ways to warn people away from the Waste Isolation Pilot Plant in southern New Mexico, where nuclear waste will be stored underground in tunnels. Assuming that languages will continue to evolve during the millennia of contamination, what imagery might be so archetypally threatening that it would scare away either the unwary or vandals seeking to plunder valuable materials from a former military installation? The architect Michael Brill proposed thirty-foot berms designed to look like thorns, but the design was rejected as being too vulnerable to interpretation as earth art. Another proposal features sculptures of nauseated faces. However, apart from deciding that granite is an appropriate material for construction (unlike the equally long-lived titanium, which might be a target for industrial scavengers), and that warnings should be inscribed on the marker in at least seven languages, a kind of nuclear Rosetta Stone, no design has yet been accepted as threatening enough to keep people away for the up to fifty thousand years it would take the materials to become safe.

All the time we're staring down into the pit, puffy white cumuli have been coalescing into dark rain clouds spreading eastward toward us from the Mount Charleston Wilderness Area, which peaks out at over 11,000 feet. On the other side of the pit, a dust devil kicks up. Thin gray curtains of virga, rain that falls but fails to reach the ground, are beginning to pull down the sky. Derek keeps us moving, this time to what he calls "the *pièce de la résistance*," the Frenchman Flat playa, which is the larger of the two dry lakes that remain within the NTS. (Groom Lake, before the Test Site boundaries were redrawn to transfer control to the Nellis Range, used to be the largest playa on the Site. It was chosen for development of Stealth aircraft, in fact, because it was the largest dry lake any distance from a public road that the air force could find in the 1950s.)

Frenchman Flat is 123 square miles in extent, however, and even from a distance it takes three photographs with a wide-angle lens to capture its breadth. It was chosen as the site for so many early aboveground tests precisely because it was large and flat enough to provide an unimpeded stage upon which to view and photograph the shots. Concrete industrial buildings, an underground parking garage doubling as a mock community shelter, steel bridge trestles, a glass house . . . parked aircraft, railroad equipment, automobiles, and military vehicles . . . even a grove of 145 ponderosa pine trees over 150 feet tall and anchored in cement were among the objects subjected to nuclear blasts at Frenchman's. The trees are long gone, but much of the other wreckage is scattered about the playa, including the empty frames of the glass house.

A 12' x 8' x 8' Mosler bank vault from San Francisco was placed on the flat for the Priscilla test in 1957, its ten-inch-thick steel door set in a steel box weighing fourteen and a half tons, which was encased in reinforced concrete several feet thick. During the same year, some 1,200 swine were kept in pens nearby, pigs having skin that most closely approximates that of humans. Anesthetized and placed at eleven stations from "2,607 to 9,405 feet from ground zero," according to Derek's guidebook, 719 of them were subjected to Priscilla. The giant Mosler safe is still there; its door still swung open after the blast. But the concrete was blown off the steel box like dirt washed off your car by a hose. Hundreds of steel rebar pieces project out on its sides, all of them bent back as if in a stiff wind. Of the pigs, only the pens remain.

I take a half dozen pictures, letting Matt and Jonathan do most of the heavy lifting on this one. I walk around the playa with my eyes on the ground, aimlessly following the cables, which are looped around in the light-brown dust like string thrown on a table. The sky is getting much darker, the wind picking up, and we instinctively head back to the Jeep, knowing that airborne particulate matter on the Site might not be the healthiest substance to inhale. As we drive up a road that rises to the west, I look back, a dust storm now obscuring the flat. I'm thinking about the pigs, and whether or not, if this were made into a park to be visited by schoolchildren, it would be child abuse to tell them about the test with the slightly old-fashioned, feminine, sweet-sounding name of Priscilla. Children make for ferocious warriors under some circumstances, so maybe it wouldn't faze them; and the research done with the pigs eventually helped the Ukrainians treat successfully those people initially harmed by the Chernobyl accident. As Matt would agree, this isn't a simple story easily converted into either a conservative rant or a liberal lecture.

The third and final part of the Test Site we visit, Jackass Flat, is mostly taken up by Area 25, which the CLUI guidebook notes is "commonly referred to as the Nevada Research and Development Area (NRDA)." Buckboard Mesa, where we found our first ground-zero this morning, is the least-impacted portion of the Test Site where nuclear tests were conducted, and Yucca the most, followed by Frenchman. Jackass Flat is an area of moderate usage, but what makes the area interesting is the variety of work carried out there, which ranges from the $6.6-billion Yucca Mountain project to abandoned MX missile silos.

Nuclear power from the 1950s onward has always been thought of by some scientists as having uses other than military ones. The Ploughshare program was one example, beating swords into instruments of cultivation being one metaphor. Project Rover, the development of nuclear rocket engines for interplanetary space travel, was another, and was tested in Area 25, as was Project Pluto, in which rocket engines were designed for terrestrial travel. There were two primary reasons for abandonment of the contemporaneous engine programs. First, it was impossible to achieve a cost-effective power-to-weight ratio in the craft, given the amount of shielding needed between the reactor and the pilot to keep him alive (and, in the 1950s through the 1970s, when these tests were being run, it was definitely not an option to the brass to have women flying such craft). Second, there was the little public-relations problem should one of the reactors fall uncontrollably back to earth.

But the testing was carried out, nonetheless—rocket engines assembled in one place then ferried up on flatcars along a twelve-mile-long railroad to the test bunkers on a hill overlooking the flat. The site is dominated by huge steel tanks encased in a metal frame, basically a chemical mixing plant, and a large gray concrete bunker. On the back side, though, where the rockets were pushed up, locked into place, and then fired, Matt and I find two observation posts. Also constructed out of massive concrete walls, and sitting on either side of the railroad track, the posts are internally folded to provide protection, we assume, for scientists. Two round windows, actually thick glass portholes several inches thick, face out of each structure toward the firing pad, which was only several yards away.

We have no idea if people were actually in the posts when the rockets were fired, or if there were only cameras behind the leaded glass, but neither of us is comfortable imagining being so close to that much power. The RADCON level posted on the fence is 15, the highest we've seen all day. On the other hand, as Matt points out, it's positively romantic, the marriage of the twentieth century's two climax technologies, aviation to nuclear power, which could have really taken us into space. It's a mood somewhat belied by the fact that the four portholes have been shot out with single, precise shots from very high-powered weapons. The only people who could safely get away with such van-dalism are probably either the Wackenhut guards or the elite armed forces personnel who train periodically on the hills nearby.

The dark skies, which we had left temporarily at Frenchman Flat, are now catching up to us, and as we drive deeper out onto Jackass Flat, I'm wondering if we'll get a thunderstorm while here, which would be my idea of a good time. It would display one apocalyptic energy against another, lightning so powerful that scientists can only compare it to nuclear explosions, the only other bright force we know of on the planet that generates that level of fury.

We pass by the BREN tower, relocated from where it held the bare nuclear reactor above Japan Town to a location where it would be out of the way, and where it is now used mostly for weather research. It's so skinny and tall that it makes no sense visually, looking like your average 350-foot-tall radio transmission tower. But in reality it's almost five times taller, and there's an elevator that goes to the top, a trip that must be harrowing on a structure so slender in comparison to its height. So many guy wires—cables, in fact—anchor its fifty-one thirty-foot segments that I can't count them without losing track. Apparently the degree of sway at the top is terrifying.

We drive almost to the Lathrop Wells gate of the Test Site, which leads out to Highway 95 and is the primary entrance point used by Yucca Mountain workers, before we head back to exit through Mercury, a retracing demanded by security. At our turn-around point, four immense concrete cylinders lie next to each other on the ground. They're so large that the Jeep could easily drive into them, and we hike inside one of them and down to its far end. It's more than eerie to be standing at the bottom plate of what was to be a silo for the proposed MX Missile Program, a steel plug more than a foot thick against which the flames of the rocket would have pushed during launch.

The MX was an idea promoted by President Reagan, and despite deep and lengthy adverse public reaction, abandoned for good only when he switched allegiance to its *doppelgänger,* the Star Wars program, which is still under development. The MX system would have placed hundreds of underground silos spread out over 25,000 square miles of Nevada and Utah. Employing 100,000 people to build and costing an estimated $100 billion at the start of construction, much less the finish, it would have been the largest building project in the history of humankind. The missiles were to have been shuffled from silo to silo by rail and special trucks (on highways massively reinforced to handle the load)—a ponderous shell game.

The space-based Star Wars would have used lasers to shoot down missiles. Its problem was the obverse of the MX; instead of a shell game featuring a few missiles and many launching sites, lasers would have had to cope with many decoys launched from only a few sites. All such defensive systems, including the current scheme to erect a fixed land-based missile shield, have similar numerical deficiencies in their logic. Countries capable of launching large strikes against a missile or laser shield would deploy numerous decoys, thus watering down the success ratio of the defense. Countries with smaller numbers of missiles would be encouraged to build more.

Looking around us at the empty valleys, which are so large that from any distance these MX silos lying on their sides appear to be a set of toy pick-up sticks, I think it's not just politics that drives leaders to push for illogical systems. It's also a severe disconnect from reality. If the visual nature of this landscape makes it hard to understand, do we suffer from a corollary dissonance in comprehending large populations in cities? It's a perceptual problem at the other end of the scale, but after all, just as we didn't evolve in deserts, neither did we do so in a hive. When calculating the cost, efficacy, and misery of nuclear war, are we simply unable to understand the vaporization of millions of people?

Energy at that scale is meaningless to us unless we see its effects in front of us. Just as we're dumbstruck in the face of large-scale natural cataclysms—tornadoes and avalanches, for example—so a nuclear explosion affects us. Walter Cronkite was reduced to silence when confronted by an example of nuclear warfare because his senses were overwhelmed. Just as we reduce the desert to cartography in order to subdivide it and build houses, a mathematics that does not address the shortage of water, so we reduce large energies and aggregates of humanity into numerical physics and demography. When Derek talks about 150 million curies of radiation on the Test Site, it's not only a meaningless number to me, it does not bring individual suffering into the equation. It's a truism that numeracy allows us to manipulate the world while abstracting ourselves away from the human consequences, but it's also a fact made tangible by what we've seen today.

By the time we finish mulling over the size of the MX weapons, which we can comprehend only through the long echoing tubes where they would have resided, it's almost five o'clock. Derek was right—we'll get back to Las Vegas about sunset. On our way out of Jackass Flats, I keep my eye on the BREN tower, the only major vertical structure visible for miles. The radio that Derek carries has just broadcast a blanket warning over the Test Site for lightning strikes and warning everyone out here—all four of us—to stay away from tall objects. As a natural hazard, versus the man-made ones around us, it's actually more reassuring than not.

A Tour of the Playa   Part III: Wendover

Three great voids upon the sphere of the earth are defined in American imagination by heat and salt and emptiness. The first and oldest in our culture is the Dead Sea, which lies within Jordan and Israel at 1,312 feet below sea level. It is the lowest and saltiest body of water on earth. Four thousand years ago, the region was a fertile agricultural area; the archaeological and geological records show that around 1900 B.C. an earthquake of sizable dimensions, perhaps accompanied by explosions of natural gas and other petroleum products, destroyed what the Bible refers to as Sodom and Gomorrah. Another, more subtle disaster awaits there today. In the last forty years, the surface of the Dead Sea has dropped 262 feet because of the diversion of 90 percent of its freshwater sources for upstream agricultural irrigation. The creation of a toxic situation similar to that at the Aral Sea seems possible.

The second is one of our own national parks and, although within California, also within the Great Basin. Death Valley, at 282 feet below sea level, is a contestant for the hottest place on the planet. Libya holds the record for the highest air temperature, 136.4°F observed in 1922, but Death Valley is only slightly lower at 134° in 1913. The American reading, however, wasn't taken at the lowest and hottest part of the valley—on the salt pan, or saline playa known as Badwater Basin—where the temperature is known to run consistently several degrees higher. In order to understand the effects of such extreme temperatures upon the human body, the American military quantified them, while fighting the Germans in North Africa during World War II, as follows: Walk around when it's 120° and you'll lose a quart of water an hour from your body through perspiration. Fail to replace the water and you can walk for a maximum of seven miles, or about two hours, before collapsing. You'll be dead within a day.

The third lacuna is the Great Salt Lake and the desert that extends westward from it. Second only to the Dead Sea in saltiness (and up to eight times as salty as the oceans), it's not below sea level yet occupies the most profound basin within the entire Great Basin, its sediments over twelve thousand feet deep in places. It is a definitive desert space by its size and the abruptness of its borders. Drive east out of Elko on Interstate 80 and come over the last pass in Nevada, a small rise just before Wendover, and the abruptness with which you enter an utterly different space is simply confounding. People driving east pause in Wendover to eat, gas up, and gamble away their last spare change before leaving behind legalized gaming—but those are all just excuses to stop and catch your breath when confronted by one of the truly big vistas in the world, sightlines of up to seventy miles being not uncommon.

The lake currently averages a surface expanse of just under 2,400 hundred square miles, the Great Salt Lake Desert of western Utah encompassing an additional 4,000 square miles. At its largest extent, the surface of its parent body of water, the Pleistocene Lake Bonneville, was more than nine hundred feet higher than today, and, as mentioned in the introduction, at nearly 20,000 square miles almost as large as Lake Michigan. When its surface elevation reached 5,090 feet some 16,800 years ago and it breached to the north in what is now Idaho to send its waters into the Snake and Columbia river systems, its outflow is estimated to have been 15 million cubic feet per second, some four to five times the discharge rate of the Amazon River. The relict Great Salt Lake remains the largest lake in the Great Basin, roughly seventy-five miles north by south and thirty-five miles wide, though that can vary dramatically during a series of wet El Niño years, its dimensions then exceeding ninety-two miles long by forty-eight miles wide in places. Its contemporary surface fluctuates around 4,200 feet in elevation, relatively stable compared to that of the Aral or Dead Seas, though there are concerns about the brine shrimp populations because industrial causeways have created disparities of water temperature and salinity in different areas of the lake.

The Great Salt Lake Desert is the largest known example of what used to be called a wet playa, one where the received waters cannot sink into the soils because of underlying layers of clay and bedrock, but are lost only through evaporation and evapotranspiration by plants. When wet, its salts are dissolved down into just below the surface and the ground appears gray or brown. When dry, the ground is white with encrusted salts, so white that to be out on it during a bright mid-day without sunglasses is to risk snowblindness.

On the western edge of the Great Salt Lake Desert, and straddling the Nevada-Utah border at an elevation of 4,500 feet on one of the ancient lake's fifty or so terraces, is Wendover, a severely schizophrenic town. On the Utah side, the older part of the community is traditionally Mormon, residential, and sliding indecorously downhill into mobile-home trailer parks for the casino workers, mostly Hispanic, who trek across the border at the beginning and end of their shifts. On the Nevada side, a half dozen high-rise casinos vie garishly for your attention, supermarkets boom, and a well-watered housing development is creeping westward, away from the border and the strictures of the Latter Day Saints. According to a count made in spring of 2000 by a local reporter, Wendover holds 146 buildings and 200 trailers.

It's on the Utah side, appropriately enough, that the CLUI's single-wide manufactured housing unit is located. Simply known as the "Unit," it's a twelve-by-seventy-foot donation from the Los Angeles Department of Wastewater Management, and the destination to which Matt Coolidge and I have driven the day after leaving the Nevada Test Site. At sunset this mid-April evening, thunderstorms are moving off to the east and lightning punctuates the horizon. A few hundred yards away, the cavernous World War II hangar for the *Enola Gay*, the plane that dropped the world's first atomic weapon, has already gathered night inside—but then, time in Wendover follows unusual rules. Utah runs on Mountain time, Nevada on Pacific, set an hour earlier; however, although the state border here is as straight as any line a surveyor could imagine, all of Wendover is on Mountain time, hosting the only clocks within Nevada to be set so. Upon arrival we're suddenly an hour later than expected, and go to bed an hour early.

Members of the Dominguez-Escalante expedition touched upon a section of west-central Utah in 1776 but didn't even see the Great

Enola Gay **hangar.** CLUI Archive

Salt Lake. It wasn't until fifty-seven years later that the region was traversed into Nevada by non-Indian travelers. A former army engineer,
Captain Bonneville, hired mountain man Joseph Walker to take a
party in 1833 past the northern shore of the Great Salt Lake, across Nevada, and into California. Frémont, while limning the Great Basin,
came through in 1843; within five years and upon publication of his
report with Preuss's map, part of the route had become one of the
principal emigrant thoroughfares of the West. Not far behind Frémont and the emigrants came yet another member of the U.S. Army
Corps of Topographical Engineers, Howard Stansbury, sent by his superiors to survey the Great Salt Lake Valley in 1849–50. The hope was
that he would find a route for the transcontinental railroad that was
being planned, and so he did, in the process surveying Promontory
Point where the western- and eastern-reaching lines would be joined
in 1869.

Stansbury, the first known Euro-American to circumnavigate the
lake, was also the person to discover that it was the prehistoric rem-

nant of "a vast *inland* sea," later to be named Lake Bonneville. (Clarence King in the 1870s would recognize that Pyramid Lake, named by Frémont, was the remnant of its sister, the Pleistocene Lake Lahontan.) Stansbury also applied triangulation for the first time in the West as a mapping technique; without the establishment of straight baselines and taking angles from prominent points around the lake, there would have been no hope of accurately surveying such a flat and featureless expanse. A courageous and persevering man, Stansbury, in traveling through the desert west of the lake, was reduced to using the words "barren" and "desolate" more than any others to describe what he saw there; "barren, desolate, and forlorn to the last degree," in fact, is one of his better combinations.

While following Walker and Frémont's trail toward Pilot Peak and Nevada during his circumlocution in November 1849, Stansbury's party passed whole wagons abandoned with their goods still inside, their wheels stuck fast in the mud. Carcasses of oxen were plentiful. He found the entire western plain of the basin to be mud, and lost several of his mules to thirst, exhaustion, and exposure to the winds from which they had difficulty finding shelter behind anything other than the occasionally taller-than-normal specimen of sagebrush. When Stansbury finished his five-thousand-square-mile survey of the basin in September 1850 and prepared to return home across the Wasatch, he recorded in his report that it was with enormous relief that his party "reached this eastern barrier of the Great Basin, in which we had been floundering amid dreary deserts and barren mud-plains for the last thirteen months."

Stansbury concluded at the end of this report that, apart from the Mormons tethering a city to the watershed of the Wasatch, the region's enormous flats were good for only one thing—accurately measuring an arc of the meridian. Determining the correct size of the earth was of paramount importance to improving navigation during the nineteenth century, and indeed a Transcontinental Triangulation Survey would be conducted across a twenty-five-hundred-mile stretch of the

39th parallel from Cape May, New Jersey, to Point Arena on the California coast. Beginning in 1871, triangulation points were established by heliotropes from mountaintop to mountaintop, and the survey finally was completed in 1898. They still didn't get it right—the size of the earth—but, as is the case with most cartography, they came closer than before.

The 39th parallel crosses Nevada roughly from Genoa in the west to Wheeler Peak in the east and is drawn across the midsection of Utah considerably south of the Great Salt Lake. Stansbury's point was valid, though. The size of the valleys in the Great Basin, and the flatness of their lake beds, was not only perfect for tracing a straight line; that was the only way they could wrap their minds around the region, by drawing and quartering it, as it were, with a mapping graticule.

The land around Wendover has been heavily redesigned since then for human usage, creating what Matt calls an "anthropic landscape," and the CLUI Unit in which we're staying sits on the northern edge of what was the largest bomber base in America during World War II. According to the CLUI guidebook to the area, *Around Wendover*, construction on the base began in 1940. Within three years, it was one of the largest military reserves in the world, housing 23,000 military personnel in 668 buildings, and training them across 3.5 million acres of the desert. By the 1950s, the air force had abandoned most of the base, later quit-claiming it to the town of Wendover, which subsequently was forced to cede it to the county when the city almost went bankrupt trying to develop it into a commercial airport for casino junkets.

Coolidge and his colleagues had never assumed they would be staying in the Culver City building with the Jurassic Museum of Technology, a property that has since been bought by the two organizations. Instead, the CLUI looked for a home elsewhere, at first considering the Baldwin Hills area in Los Angeles. Featuring numerous inactive construction sites, it fit the CLUI criteria for a place that had undergone successive layers of industrial land use, but the deal never got off the ground. Wherever the CLUI was going to be located, Matt and friends knew they wanted satellite locations; what attracted them to Wendover was precisely its multiple and overlapping patterns of human usage, which were historically much denser than those in Baldwin Hills. Besides emigrants, its transportation corridor had been used by the first transcontinental railroad, highway, and telephone lines. In addition to the modern-day Goshute tribe, prehistoric peoples had lived nearby in Danger Cave as long ago as ten thousand years before the present. It was a military, mining, industrial, and tourism site—and it had the requisite air of dead technology that is a hallmark of millennial aesthetics.

The CLUI has been in Wendover since 1996, when it opened an exhibition hall in a former barracks building located north of the Unit. In 1997 the organization began hosting artists' residencies in a nearby studio, putting up visitors in the trailer that now sits next to the Unit and serves as a spare bedroom. The Unit itself was trucked to Wendover and installed on a freshly poured concrete slab only last year. Housing artists and writers for periods ranging from a week to six weeks throughout the months of May through November, the Unit not only institutionalizes the CLUI practice of sponsoring artists to work in the desert but expands upon an existing local artistic heritage, albeit a mostly contemporary one. Because the Great Salt Lake Desert is so large, flat, and remote, it has attracted extreme forms of usage not as visible elsewhere, the airbase among them. As a result, notable photographers have been drawn to the area for years, among them Stuart Klipper (1941–) and Richard Misrach.

Klipper, an articulate and witty artist from Minneapolis, has spent much of his life photographing landscapes with a panoramic camera. About the size and heft of three conventional 35-mm rangefinders, it is carried in his padded bag wherever he goes, including on several trips to the Antarctic, by far the world's largest and most extreme desert. Klipper is working in a tradition that reaches back to seventeenth-century Dutch landscape art, which in part arises from an even earlier practice of sailors making topographically explicit panoramas of the coasts they were following in order to relocate safe harbors and identify shoals. Their coastal profiles, which usually appeared in their pilot logs, or "rutters," were necessary for survival along what is essentially a flat coast with no prominent verticalities to act as landmarks. Water also penetrated the Netherlands' interior through extensive canals and lakes, and the coastal profiles soon morphed into panoramic landscapes, which remains a strong genre in both photography and painting today.

The photographs that Klipper makes hold our vision even when they contain no vertical figures upon which to focus our attention, doing so by the ways in which Klipper capitalizes upon the virtue of their horizontal stretch. You find your entire head moving from side to side in an attempt to read the horizon in his pictures, eventually slowing down to admire the subtleties of the ground itself. The pictures he took on the Bonneville Raceway, just eight miles east of town, during the winter of 1990, are perfect examples. The flats are flooded with gray water; the sky is flooded with gray clouds; the horizon is defined more by where they imperceptibly meet than by any landform. Klipper, in allowing himself to photograph almost nothing figurative, gets the cognitive dissonance of the Big Empty exactly right.

The relationship between photographer and playa has been more explored by Richard Misrach than perhaps anyone else. Contemporary photographers working in the West now routinely shoot the playas, a landform that is no longer so unfamiliar to viewers as to appear either uninteresting or unappealing, but the artists do so mostly within only a narrow band of the full aesthetic spectrum. The twentieth-century traditionalist Philip Hyde, for example, excludes from his photographs all traces of human activity on the playas, and thus pictures them as a romantic ideal in the manner of Ansel Adams. Peter Goin, who teaches at the University of Nevada, Reno, tends to take his playa photographs at midday, flattening out the territory into what he considers to be an objective, but tightly constrained, view.

What Misrach brings to the subject that is unique is a structured way of integrating it into a larger framework of desert imagery, working within what he calls his desert "cantos," named after the Ezra Pound poems. The Italian term means a subdivision of an epic poem, which Pound meant, in turn, to refer back to Dante's use of cantos in *The Divine Comedy*. Cantos are to an epic poem as chapters are to a novel, allowing the artist to sustain a very long arc in his work that keeps everything perceptible as parts within a whole.

Misrach started photographing seriously in the desert in 1975; many of the landscapes that he took in 1979 would in 1983, after reading a book on Pound's work, be organized into *Desert Canto I: The Terrain*. He was already photographing the sandy desert floor as part of his working visual vocabulary, and many of his photographs in various cantos were taken on playas. *Canto II: The Event*, which documented a landing of the space shuttle, is set on Rogers Dry Lake. His 1983 photo of the landing site is one of the blankest and most straightforward playa photos I've ever seen, displaying perfectly the desiccated floor, the far shoreline, and beyond that the mountains that form the requisite rain shadow. The rest of that series, much of which is devoted to the deployment of the spectators and their vehicles, demonstrates how military and civilian cultures come together in the desert—a theme that underlies much of Misrach's work and is visibly evident on many of the major playas not only in North America but also on those falling within the jurisdiction of that other Cold War superpower, the former Soviet Union.

In the case of *Canto III: The Flood*, which uses the Salton Sea as its subject, he's photographing an anomalous example of the genre: a once-dry lake that is now the largest standing body of water in the state of California, the result of a broken dike allowing the Colorado River to flood a desert valley almost a century ago. *Canto VIII: The Event II*, taken in the 1990s during several of the annual celebrations of Burning Man, is on the Black Rock Desert. *Canto XV: The Salt Flats*, done in 1992–93, is about the Bonneville Speedway, where cars had been setting land-speed records since 1914. The five-foot-thick surface layer of salt was first evened out by dragging a land plane over it, and then ruled off with an eleven-mile-long line of black motor oil. This, too, was a kind of performance target, only instead of being a bull's-eye for bombs it was a ruler against which to measure speed. Misrach's photos poise at rest on the salt flats whatever was designed to be mobile—from a person on rollerblades to the world's fastest motor home—thus reducing the idea of speed to a thunderous silence.

Misrach came to Wendover repeatedly from 1986 through 1991 to work on *Canto IX: The Secret (Project w-47)*, which documents the landscape just south and immediately outside the front door of the CLUI Unit. "Project w-47" was the designation given to the training program for the atomic-bomb crews, which practiced loading dummy weapons into and dropping them from the *Enola Gay*. He took exterior shots of the playa from within the ordnance area known as South Base, which is a few hundred yards away from the Unit, photographs that situate the ammo bunkers and a miscellany of military wreckage in the middle of not only the vast desolation that so plagued Stansbury but also within a variety of atmospheric conditions. At times he worked when the light was bright, harsh, and not far from flat, but at others within a late-afternoon golden light under low gray skies that appear to the viewer to be suspiciously dramatic. Suspicious, that is, until you're in Wendover in spring and see those same conditions appearing day after day.

The interiors that Misrach filmed, including the *Enola Gay* hanger, have suffered extensive vandalism since he was last here, but traces remain of the military graffiti adorning the walls, such as the crudely painted mushroom cloud in an administrative building, a picture that encloses the words "Eat My Fallout" written in red. What haunts the old airbase, despite the somewhat tattered but still intact shrouds of secrecy, is a palpable sense that history was made here, a history of which the now-deceased men and women fighting in a global war were proud. It's another example of the way in which time here has gone strange.

Awakening at 6:30 a.m. on the first day of our stay in Wendover, I fumble my way out of the rear bedroom of the CLUI Unit. After negotiating the unfamiliar and strikingly industrial interior of the Unit, which was designed and decorated by the SIMPARCH architectural firm of New Mexico, I go outside, stretch, and gently tap the nose cone of an Intercontinental Ballistic Missile sitting inexplicably next to the door. Finding a gap in the chain-link fence, I slip through and head for a walk around the airfield. Matt is still asleep, so I take for my immediate goal a tall red kiosk about the size of a phone booth standing next to a tree, one of the CLUI artists' projects. The air is cool after yesterday's storm, and already to the west small cumuli are building, presaging another round of thunderstorms later in the day. A lone pickup truck drives around the recently restored runways of the airfield, which now support a modest amount of sporadic small aircraft traffic.

To my left, early-morning sunlight streams horizontally into the *Enola Gay* hangar, shining on what look to be the tail ends of several gas-tanker semi-trailer trucks parked inside. The *Enola Gay*, a B-29 bomber, was named by its commander, Colonel Paul Tibbets, for his mother. "Little Boy" was the first atomic bomb to be dropped on Japan, a gun-type uranium device released from the *Enola Gay* at 31,600 feet. It was 12:01 P.M. on August 9, 1945, and within minutes the city of Hiroshima was flattened by the thirteen-kiloton explosion, which was designed to burst in the air at 1,300 feet above the city in order to maximize the immediate destruction. Seventy thousand people died from the blast, not counting later deaths from radiation exposure. The destruction was biblical in its proportions.

Parked out on the runway to one side of the *Enola Gay* hangar is an oddly truncated dummy of an airplane surrounded by a modest fence. A prop from the action movie *Con Air*, which featured a gang of escaped convicts hijacking their aerial transport, it's actually mounted on a bus chassis. It fell on a crew member while it was being assembled and killed him, and because the accident took place at a working airport, law required that the Federal Aviation Administration be called in, its officials subsequently insisting that the prop be parked, fenced, and supervised as if it were a real aircraft. The fake airplane sitting on a runway used to launch the *Enola Gay* on its mission is a juxtaposition surreal even by Hollywood standards.

The *Con Air* production company used Wendover as a stand-in location for a remote landing field in the Central Valley of California, and part of the science-fiction movie *Independence Day* was also filmed here, using the playa to represent Groom Lake. A few years earlier, *Mulholland Falls* had used the local desert for a Nevada Test Site sequence. Debris from *Con Air* still litters part of South Base, and in fact the film crew went so far as to erect a nearly exact duplicate of the historical control tower by the ammo bunkers down there. Too far to walk to this morning; I'll save that for later, as well as exploring the hangar.

The red kiosk I'm walking toward is one of *Five Interpreted Views: An Obscura Excursion* erected by L.A. artist Jeremy Kunkle in 1998. Matt isn't sure how many of the five installations, which were scattered around the area, including the bombing range to the south, still remain. Although the military at first assumed they were somehow connected with the secret development of Stealth aircraft technology and left them alone, eventually they called in intelligence experts and deciphered that they were, in fact, something else. What, they weren't exactly sure, but they have dismantled at least three of them and left behind small signs listing a phone number to call for anyone trying to locate the missing installations.

What I find, when I reach it, is a light-tight booth built of plywood with a spring-loaded door that closes upon a matte-black interior. Standing inside, my eyes adjusting to the darkness, an image of the tree outside slowly emerges to my left on the surface of a ground-glass plate. The floating picture of the tree leafing out in front of the playa is a delicate and ghostly anomaly. I walk back outside, go around the booth by the tree, and find the small pinhole through which light pen-

Camera obscura from *Five Interpreted Views: An Obscura Excursion* by Jeremy Kunkle. *Enola Gay* hangar in background. CLUI Archive

etrates the wall to form the image inside. The principle of the camera obscura has been known at least since Aristotle in the fourth century B.C., who observed that the round shape of the sun was projected as a disk on the ground as light passed through woven wicker, even though the interstices of the cane were angular. The device became popular in Europe during the eighteenth century, first as room-sized enclosures one could enter—like Kunkle's installation—and then as progressively smaller instruments. Conventional modern cameras are, in a way, nothing more than miniaturizations designed to fix permanently the image produced by the earlier version of the same device.

Still walking around the booth, I find another pinhole, although I'd not observed a second image inside, and I reenter to locate it. Bending the light path with a mirror, Kunkle has produced a picture of the hanger, which floats horizontally below my chest. Pondering the reversal of the image, which has been rotated by the mirror, I notice to my surprise that the image is in color. Looking over at the image of the tree, I see that it too is in color, a pale but distinct green. I'd automatically preconceived what I was going to see as black and white, categorizing the experience beforehand as an anachronistic one produced by a technology dating from before the invention of color film, when in fact there's no film involved.

Some cognitive scientists now think that what we see is composed of about equal parts external stimuli and internal mental responses. Visual information streaming into the brain is met and processed by not only an array of neurological responses, such as boundary and pattern recognition, but is also restructured by memory and learned expectations. We see what we expect to see, in other words, which is related to why it's easy for us to finish words and sentences with missing letters and even entire phrases. Yet another version of visual dissonance, it seems an instructive way to begin a day in the desert.

Once again outside the booth, I decide to keep walking east out toward what Matt had told me the evening before is a new drag strip. I enter by way of the rear pit area, where the cars are pushed into their starting position. Tiny black fragments of shredded tires are spalled behind the starting line, detritus from the dragsters peeling out. The smell of scorched rubber hangs faintly in the air. Utilizing part of an old runway not currently in service, a center line divides the concrete path in front of me into two parallel tracks for the competing cars. It disappears toward the classic vanishing point of the desert, and I walk out the length of the timed quarter mile. Toward the end of the course I have the sensation, as in everyone's favorite recurring dream, that if I just stretched out my arms a little I would lift into the air and start to fly.

By the time I return to the Unit, Matt has risen, if not into the air, at least into the kitchen, and made coffee. After some heavy caffeine-loading, he takes me over to the exhibition hall across the road to the north so I can examine photographs of other CLUI art projects while he begins to determine what his maintenance chores will be for the next two days.

Only twenty-four of the more than six hundred structures remain from the war, all of them enclosed by a locked fence, most of them leased for various uses by local individuals and firms. They house everything from designers of computerized knitting machines to autobody repair shops. The CLUI building is typical—a small office at one end, then a long handsome room with exposed beams under a peaked roof. Everything is painted a light institutional green, now coated with dust. Suspended from the center of the open ceiling joists and running the length of the room are the exhibit panels.

The first CLUI artist to be in residence here was Alice Konitz from Germany, who came in 1997. Intrigued with Wendover, she had approached the organization eighteen months previously about working there, and the program was actually designed with Konitz specifically in mind. In her late twenties and working as what Matt calls a "materials conceptualist," she wrangled a donation of salt from Reilly Industries, the local saltworks, and made sculptures out of the mineral, which were allowed to melt gradually away in the weather. "The irony of salt and snow—" Matt comments as I walk about the photographs, "they kill each other and make water."

The next year, John Reed came from San Diego with his friend Jennifer Odem from Texas. They collaborated to create autonomous, wind-propelled kinetic sculptures that are actually drawing machines. Riding on anything from three to twelve wheels that leave traces of their passage on the flats, the sculptures were constructed in California out of tubular metal to be powered as if they were, variously, windmills, box kites, and propeller-driven craft. The two artists let them loose on sections of the salt flats bounded by road embankments and flood berms, thus ensuring that they wouldn't get in the way of anyone.

Occasionally an off-roader or BLM official will come across one or more that have gotten stuck in a dead end, and the artists will receive an amused phone call. John and Jennifer drive back up to reorient the machines and set them to wandering once more, sometimes taking older models back with them and releasing new ones. The photos show the machines to be just intricate and unusual enough in appearance to be intriguing, and I'd love to see one, but Matt has no idea where they might be currently, that being part of the point, of course. They remind me of more delicate, less gloomy, roving versions of the Tinguely machines, though their intent is radically optimistic compared to his staged end-of-the-world happening.

Just prior to Kunkle, Kelly Coyne had been in residence, launching small hobby rockets that, while pausing at their apogee and just before parachuting back to earth, snapped blurry pictures of the ground. Abstracted enough from any direct consideration of rocketry so that it's possible to consider the photos artistic, versus merely political, yet a poised reminder of the buzz bombs developed on the base during the war, I found the small snapshots seductive, tempted by each one to decipher features on the ground below.

Other CLUI artists who have resided in Wendover include the photographers Sara Irving and Mark Ruwedel, the latter's photographs often appearing in CLUI publications. And Jim Harbison of San Francisco, who has been out once and will be returning, has been working on test models for his *Wall of Clang*, which the exhibition notes is a "scrap metal aeolian sculptural fence" on the state border—found metal objects suspended in air, some light enough to bang and chime in the wind, some so heavy they require a human push to activate them.

These contemporary artists are informed by, following in the path of, and extending the work of Misrach and Klipper, taking in a wide view of the world in a literal and metaphorical sense. The two photographers, in turn, were standing on the shoulders of the painters who first came West. Thomas Moran (1837–1926) was functioning in the grand romantic European tradition when painting his *Sunset on the Great Salt Lake* in 1877, a panoramic pictorialism that had become a

(above and opposite) **Wind-propelled drawing devices by John Reed and Jennifer Odem.**
Photos by Jennifer Odem

theater of exaggeration in an effort to match the scenic climaxes of the Old World. This was a method of picturing territory that had a lineage extending back through the English artists. Moran had studied closely the work of England's greatest landscape painter, J. M. W. Turner (1775–1851), who earlier had himself trained as a topographical draftsman late in the eighteenth century. Before him was William Hodges (1744–1797), a classically trained landscapist who became a talented topographer while serving as the official artist on Captain James Cook's second voyage to the South Seas in the 1770s, and who went on to become the most widely traveled artist of his century, documenting everything from Antarctic icebergs to the crumbling palaces of India. Before Hodges came the "Golden Century" of Dutch landscape painting, a school that heavily influenced the English, and that first arose, in part, out of those coastal profiles drawn by the Dutch navigators of the sixteenth century.

European landscape painting has had two major traditions to follow. To drastically oversimplify, there was a southern, or Italian, school that centered around Claude Lorrain, which demanded that landscape be organized through a set of ideal principles. A dark foreground was to be followed by a lighter midground, followed by a darker background. The scene—and scenery it was—should be framed by buildings or trees, and figures near a water feature such as a pond or river were desirable. This was a style of picturing the world that lent itself to calming allegories derived from classical mythology, and was considered the height of Continental sophistication. It was also a codified version of the terrain in which humans had evolved.

By contrast, the northern, or predominantly Dutch, pictorial tradition tended to hew much more to the practicalities of the actual land- and seascapes. The associated counties that make up what we now call the Netherlands were a vibrant commercial culture in contemplation of an open ocean, versus an established society perched above the enclosed sea of the Mediterranean. The Dutch were, by the 1600s, the greatest cartographers in the world, sending out ships to explore

Wall of Clang **by James Harbison.** CLUI Archive

those vast areas of the globe that were still unknown, a role the English would assume in the following century. Explorers prior to the invention of the camera needed accurate representation of what they found, which meant both maps and topographically accurate coastal profiles and landscapes enabling them to find their way back to safe harbors. Look at even the domestic scenes painted by Vermeer (1632–1675), and you'll often find maps hanging in the background, so venerated were they by Dutch society. It was a pictorial tradition developed in response and out of necessity to landscapes, from the tropical to the arctic, that were newly discovered and distinctly foreign to our evolved visual programming.

As landscapes become more known, pictorial or literal representation tends to give way to symbolic transformation, our need to infuse into nature a spirituality that is above and beyond us, a longstanding trait we developed in order to withstand the perceived chaos of the universe. We constantly organize space around us not only through mathematical grids but also into more subtle psychological channels that manifest themselves as a taste for religion and the sublime in art. Moran can be seen as a bridge figure in the West, painting real landscapes but attempting to elevate them into symbols representing a great and ineffable reality at the limits of our vision. Photographers such as Timothy O'Sullivan were taking care of the topographical needs, which the American audience appreciated, but a market for pictures that attempted to represent the spirit of the sublime in nature also existed, which only a painter could fulfill.

The audience for such theatrical views eventually paled, the romantic panoramas not only falling out of a cycle of style but also overwhelmed by the grim existential realities of the First World War. By the time Moran died, his huge canvases of Yellowstone and the Grand Canyon, as well as Albert Bierstadt's views of the Rocky Mountains and the Sierra, had been superseded, at least in the eyes of the art-going public, by a variety of more abstract styles. It wouldn't be until almost the end of the twentieth century that such works would again find favor, and then less as great art and more as important historical documents.

Looking at work by Misrach, you'll see how often he photographs within that warm light of the late-afternoon "Golden Hour," that daily period of long shadows and glowing air of which Moran and Bierstadt also took advantage, and a light favored by the Italian classicists two centuries earlier. And it's clear that Klipper also has a keen appreciation for the extended panoramas painted and photographed throughout the history of exploration in both the Old and New Worlds. Both artists are aware of how they work from—not merely within—those traditions. Misrach, for instance, writes candidly of his political viewpoints and the meta-narrative of his *Cantos,* and Klipper can discuss the history of cartography and its relationship to photography with ease.

The CLUI artists, however, are pushing far beyond a topographical depiction of landscape. Kunkle, for example, in constructing his camera obscura booths on a bombing range, is not only picking up the most literal picture possible of the land, he's also installing a political and environmental statement, counterpoising artistic valuation of land versus its use as a target for high explosives, using the oldest cameralike device known, as opposed to the ultra-high-speed movie cameras the military deploys to record its deeds. Reed and Oden, by creating sculptures that respond to the elements in order to inscribe the land with gestures that the same elements will also erase, are in essence writing a trope on the land about the nature of a tabula rasa, the blank tablet that we assume nature, and not just playas, must be for our musings.

Before leaving the exhibition hall for a drive out onto the Bonneville Salt Flats, the road that Stuart Klipper photographed in 1990, I remember to ask Matt about a circle I saw when I'd walked out to the end of the drag strip. It had looked to me like a dozen or so telephone poles had been planted out beyond the runways in some sort of "phonehenge."

"Lightning," he replied. "The military wanted to find out what effect lightning had on Intercontinental Ballistic Missiles, so they set up the telephone poles to attract it, and ran cables from them to a missile they put in the middle. I think that's where the nose cone by the Unit came from."

It's not enough that the bunkers at South Base remind me of Michael Heizer's *Complex One*, the mastaba-like edifice that was the first element in his *City* project, but now there's a military predecessor to Walter De Maria's *Lightning Field* in New Mexico. His one-mile-long by one-kilometer-wide plantation of four hundred stainless-steel rods spread out on a grid is often pictured on the cover of art history books, lightning flashing down from a thunder-dark sky to strike the rods (or, some say, just the hills behind in a trick of perspective). Never mind trying to sort out the influences of Dutch coastal profiles on the photographic traditions of the late twentieth century; just the muddied track record of earthworks in the American Southwest is enough to baffle the audience.

The asphalt two-lane road out to the Salt Flats is another of those vanishing-point numbers, a long reddish-gray line that arrows into the horizon. On either side of us, the surface of the ground goes from a dirty brown to a gleaming white, then disappears under a shallow layer of astonishingly transparent celadon water. Today the road ends at a circular turn-around. If the flats were dry, this would be the jumping-off point where you would leave the pavement and set tire to salt. Now, however, the land sits underwater for as far as we can see eastward. By July, the flats are usually so dry they're set up like concrete, a state of hardness they maintain until November when the winter storm season begins. It's during those months that people broke land-speed records, starting in 1914, when the fastest car on earth hit 141.73 miles per hour, through 1965, when Craig Breedlove blew past 600 mph. By 1983, the real action had moved to the Black Rock Desert, the salt here being so depleted by nearby mining that the surface layer had thinned from eighteen inches deep to less than half an inch, an insufficiently strong surface to support the ever-increasing weight of the vehicles, which had come to resemble supersonic jets on wheels more than automobiles.

Out on the horizon in front of us is Floating Island, quite real though it looks like a mirage, a reverse of the optical illusion so familiar in the desert. It looks like we could swim to it, but it's sixteen miles away. Matt once took off his shoes and went wading in the shallow water. He says it's like walking on coral, the salt crust is so hard. I judge the water to be no more than three inches deep, until Matt points out a Budweiser Light bottle sitting on the bottom. The water is at least twice as deep as I'd thought; because of a lack of organic material, the water is so clear that it's hard to gauge—the liquid equivalent of desert air so dry that we have trouble visually measuring distance.

In summer, the eleven-mile-long black line is still drawn out for racers, a piece of geometry significant enough in both size and culture that, even though it's a perennial and not a permanent feature of the landscape, its position is shown on the USGS topo map. The BLM Salt Lake Field Office issues its annual allotment of forty or so permits to advertising companies and filmmakers so they can capture speeding cars for fun and profit—this, too, being a perennial event.

The 4,000-square-mile Great Salt Lake Desert that we're standing in is part of the ancient floor of Bonneville Lake, a highly provisional state of ground exemplified best by the behavior of the Great Salt Lake itself. Look up facts about the lake in books and on the Internet, and you find statements that it's the thirty-third largest lake in the world, a deceptively solid-sounding fact. In 1963, the lake was at its historically lowest level, 4,191.35 feet, and it covered only 950 square miles. In 1986–87, at its highest, it stood at 4,211.85 feet and covered 2,500 square miles. At its maximum, the lake is only thirty-three feet deep and averages more like thirteen feet, hence the immense variation in its coverage—the water rises a couple of feet and covers a few additional hundreds of square miles because of the flatness of the terrain. It loses 2.9 million acre-feet of water to evaporation each year, its water and salt both replenished by runoff from the mountains and rainfall, an exchange that statistically is seldom if ever likely to be in a state of equilibrium. For the sake of comparison, where we're parked at the end of the paved road is at 4,214 feet; the lake would have to rise only twenty-five and one quarter inches to expand from its current shoreline to here, almost sixty miles distant.

The saltiness of the lake, and of these waters at our feet this morning, depends upon climatic conditions from year to year. The lake over the horizon holds something between an estimated 4.5 to almost 5 billion tons of salt. The percentage of salt to water can range from as low as 5 percent salt, at which stage you're barely floating, to as high as nearly 27 percent, the point beyond which water can't hold salt—and you can't sink no matter how hard you try.

What I mean to say is that the numbers have trouble holding. They are always approximate, change from day to day and from one area of the lake to another, depending on the circulation of the waters, particularly as they are interrupted by the embankments of the railroad and interstate freeway. The same is true here at the Bonneville Salt Flats. As we drive back to the shoreline, we pass the edge of the water, which tomorrow will be just a little farther to the east.

It's already a half hour past noon when we reach the shore. Instead of bearing back left and south to Wendover, we turn right on a dirt road that will take us up and over Leppy Pass toward Pilot Peak, and into that part of the Great Salt Lake Desert that the Donner-Reed Party passed through on its way to a wintry fate in the frozen Sierra. Behind us is Interstate 80, a road that passes both Wendover and where the Donner Party camped in the Sierra.

We drive through Leppy Pass and take a great curving line that bends eastward under the 10,000-foot-high peak that was the mark the emigrants made for when crossing the desert, knowing that if they reached it, they would find water and then be able to find their way to the Ruby Mountains in Nevada and hence to the headwaters of the Humboldt River, which would take them more than halfway across that state. Of course, once that modest stream petered out in yet another series of dry lakes, they were faced with crossing the Forty Mile Desert outside Fallon, the deadliest playas of them all.

We have our own worries today, however, as Matt steers the van into progressively rougher terrain. We've gone from the interstate to a two-lane blacktop, then onto a dirt road that led us to an intermittent jeep track so rough that we lost the rear half of the exhaust pipe and the muffler. Finally, this washboarded and washed-out set of ruts ended at the edge of another playa, and despite the fact that showers have been building up all afternoon and now obscure the top of Pilot Peak with snow squalls, we venture out onto it. We're violating the most basic rule of playa travel, which is not to risk it when precipitation threatens, but emboldened by the fact that we have gallons of water with us, food enough for a couple of days, and, most important, a cell phone, we go for it. And the object of such self-absorbed foolishness? The original piece of property bought by Robert Smithson before he built *Spiral Jetty* in 1970 at a site clear across the lake.

Introduced to the desert by Michael Heizer the year before, and apparently ready to jump on a hot bandwagon—"earthworks" being a newly minted movement—Smithson went looking for a piece of land all his own on which he could erect a sculpture, a response to Heizer's and De Maria's works on the playas of the Mojave and the huge twin cuts of *Double Negative*.

What we find two hours after leaving pavement, and after the playa gets too soft to drive on any further, forcing us to continue briefly on foot, is a stunning piece of ranch land situated on a lake terrace above the playa. It feels like it's an open stage, the level bench framed by the small mountain range that rises behind us as we look outward onto an expanse in which there is no visible evidence of human intervention or artifact, a relatively rare occurrence underneath airspace claimed by the military as an operations area. Smithson chose well. Comparing the maps with the mountain ranges we can see, we gauge we're able to look about fifty miles east, south, and west. That's fifteen hundred square miles of clear sightline, much of it flat playa.

The artist chose not to design a sculpture for this remote arena, but instead built his gigantic rock spiral nearly a hundred miles east on the edge of Promontory Point for reasons noted earlier—the industrial nature of the other site and its steep shoreline. Projecting out into the lake, the inward-curving causeway is now underwater, which Smithson hadn't anticipated, though visible as a shape from the air. As a sculpture, the symbol lifted from petroglyphs of the region is no match for works by others working at a large scale during the latter third of the century. Heizer and Richard Serra, to name two, one working with earth and the other with steel, have carved out entire new vocabularies of space, while Smithson was more interested in exploring the theoretical implications of entropy, the laws governing how energy dissipates, and for which the spiral is an appropriate symbol. But *Spiral Jetty,* much to the dismay of Heizer, is endlessly reproduced in photographs and has also elicited a strong response from most of us, perhaps more because it extends a barren shoreline with a large abstract form than because of any artistic reason. It's a bold gesture, nonetheless, and very much part of the history of playa works.

What we're doing here is more than just exercising idle curiosity in an obscure art-historical fact. The property is owned by Nancy Holt, the sculptor and Smithson's widow. When the CLUI was looking around Wendover a couple of years ago for a site that was relatively untouched by human usage, in order to establish a baseline from which the artists could measure their work, they stumbled across it. Holt proved amenable to leasing the parcel to the organization, and Matt wanted to find out how accessible the property was this spring. He'd only been out here once before, last year, and has decided, given our experience in the van, that they need someone to donate a four-wheel-drive vehicle. Coming here without one would be too risky for the artists, most of whom aren't accustomed to desert travel. Finding a setting in which someone can work within a more obviously geological context than was available in Wendover means that they have to cope with said geology. And speaking of which, the rain is continuing to fall around us, though not yet on the playa, so we decide it's time to go.

As a footnote to the excursion, we pass the turnoff to another well-known piece of earth art, Nancy Holt's *Sun Tunnels,* four huge sections of concrete culvert into which holes were drilled to correspond to selected constellations. The twenty-two tons of pipe were aligned in the desert as an open X in 1976, their ends facing the rising and setting of the sun during the winter and summer solstices. They also provide the only shade available for miles out on the open plain. From the dirt road, although the pipes are more than nine feet in diameter and eighteen feet long, you can't tell what they are, and the first time I came to visit them in 1989, I drove by the turnoff after staring directly at them. In a typical case of dissonance, I'd thought that they were small weathered logs, which in turn reminds me of how small the MS missile silos appeared on the Test Site, larger versions of concrete pipes lying on the ground.

By the time we return to Wendover at 5 P.M., having made a hundred-mile-long circle around Pilot Peak, the rain has stopped, but the sky remains capped by heavy gray clouds. To the west there is a thin band of clear sky, which promises a clearing-off later in the evening. Matt has promised me a tour of South Base, which he appears to be anticipating with some relish. I soon see why.

We drive out along the western edge of the airfield and beyond the runways to the fences surrounding the half-dozen remaining buildings and eight bunkers. Matt unlocks a gate and we enter, our first goal being to gain the vantage point from atop the replica of the old control tower erected by the *Con Air* crew, a three- or four-story climb up rickety metal stairs to a wooden platform. The breakaway railing on top is attached only with bailing wire, and the floor is not supported underneath in places, so we walk gingerly around its perimeter, scanning the horizon.

East, the playa disappears into cloud. Supposedly you can see the curvature of the earth from here, a fallacy, but we can see indirect evidence of it—when it's clear you can't see the bottoms of the mountains in that direction, only their tops. South, the burned-out hulk of a car used by SWAT teams and local firemen on which they practice their craft sits by the fence. The low berm belonging to the Reilly Industries saltworks stretches out for ten miles before curving east and disappearing. That's it. The flat goes for seventy miles until it ends at the Fish Spring and Thomas ranges, the tops of what I think must be the latter still holding snow. West, the slopes of the Toana Range in Nevada recede in misty layers. North, Wendover spreads out, a low fan of buildings splayed out below the mostly invisible interstate.

We don't stay topside for long because it's breezy and cool, and we climb back down to visit two buildings that the CLUI rents for storage.

"It's just a toehold," Matt says with a shrug. "What we'd really like to have is this whole part of the base. We'd move most of our operations out here and leave behind the exhibition hall as a public portal. But there's no running water, electricity, or sewage here, which would be expensive. And it would be hard to find a funder who would understand that what we would do here wouldn't be typical historical preservation but more like what they're doing in the Rühr Valley of Germany, where they're recycling industrial plants into cultural facilities."

Matt keeps talking as we walk around the buildings taking pictures. "South Base is where they worked on munitions away from the planes and barracks. You can see some of the graffiti that Misrach photographed, though it's disappearing pretty fast." Sure enough, we find a mushroom cloud, along with "Ammo: We live so others may die" and "If you ain't ammo, you ain't shit." All of it strikes me as less military machismo and more the braggadocio of people working voluntarily under the constant threat of extinction from their task at hand, a feeling that's reinforced when we drive among the bunkers. Those with doors facing the airfield and town have high berms faced with thick concrete constructed in front of them as blast shields. Those facing south and into the desert don't. It's an economy of time and material: protect the airplanes and their super-secret, delicate Norden bombsights. For the personnel working in the bunkers, there was no protection possible. A brave face, some crude humor, a lot of heavy lifting done very carefully. Nowadays, local businesses use the bunkers to store their junk.

"This is a nationally significant site, don't you think?" Matt asks. "I mean, this could be an art proving-ground on par with anything else in the country." I agree, noting that without active usage the cycles of salt, water, and wind will simply wear it down. During the war, the military supposedly constructed an entire mock city out of salt out on the flats, a target for bombing practice. Matt's never been able to locate it on a map, much less see it, and presumes it must have melted away by now. The effect here will be the same; the materials here are a little more resistant, the process slower, but entropy won't be denied unless someone uses and maintains the facility.

Now we leave South Base and venture out farther onto the playa, driving on an elevated berm that's more what Matt calls "a peninsula" than a road. "I don't know where else you can be on land and feel so much like you're on water," he observes. At the end we stop to examine the foundations for a long-since-salvaged elevated track that was used to launch unguided missiles southward, American buzz bombs that were a cruder version of the German v-1 rockets targeted for London.

"I think it's interesting," Matt continues, "that there's a history of rocketry here. They were developing the technology to go into space in a place that's the most like outer space in the country." This is a constant refrain you bump up against in the most arid, most absolute desert spots, from the bottom of the Sedan Crater, to here, to Meteor Crater in Arizona, to the Dry Valleys of the Antarctic: their use as analog environments for space exploration. All of them have been used to test either rockets or extraterrestrial vehicles, or to train astronauts, who wander around in their white suits. Not far from Smithson's *Spiral Jetty* is the Thiokol complex, where the rocket engines powering the space shuttle are made. Utah and Nevada are rife with amateur, commercial, and military rocketry.

Turning around, we backtrack to a spur that leads to what looks like a fairly recent crater. Almost three yards across and several feet deep, it's filled with scummy rainwater.

"Veterans get together to come out here in rebuilt vintage planes and drop homemade bombs. I don't think the military would be bombing this close to town anymore, so maybe this is one of theirs." In order to get a photograph of the shallow hole, Matt clambers to the platform anchored to the roof of the van, a custom amenity many photographers who work in the desert install atop their vehicles. It's one of the few ways you can organize large flat spaces around you, by gaining elevation, a trick Frémont knew well and that allowed him to discern the nature of the Great Basin, climbing up the Wasatch and looking west, then up the northernmost Sierra and looking east. This more modest ascent of Matt's puts his lens almost twelve feet above the ground, just enough so the crater fills out from a two- into a three-dimensional feature.

Leaving the van by the crater, we decide to hike over to the berm I'd seen from the tower. Perhaps five feet high from this side, it turns out to be one side of a channel. Inside, it's almost twice as deep. Running south by southwest and carrying a wide but shallow flow of water, the bottom of the trench is visibly below the grade of the playa floor. Because layers of clay beneath the accumulated salt and alkali prevent rainwater and runoff from percolating deep into the ground, the surface waters sink down only a few inches and bear their loads of dissolved salts and minerals laterally across the desert. Meeting the trench, the water flows in and down to where Reilly Industries pumps the water into evaporation ponds. As the ponds dry out, enormous articulated earthmovers scrape up the salt deposits and lumber back with them to the processing plant, which is easily visible from most of Wendover.

The first saltworks were established in the area in 1914, then moved to the current location twelve years later, an 88,000-acre property the chemical company acquired in the 1980s. Reilly, a large corporation that makes everything from B-3 vitamins to DEET, the active ingredient in most insect repellents, prides itself on its large-scale efficiencies, which dramatically altered the environmental balance of the playa. Raking up a little salt around the midcentury didn't hurt the Bonneville Salt Flats much, but Reilly now extracts 850,000 tons of salt per year to produce 100,000 tons of potash, a substance used primarily in fertilizers. Another salty byproduct is magnesium chloride, which is used in products to control ice on roads and suppress dust.

Figure that one ton of salt takes up about a cubic yard, that the company measures its evaporation ponds by counting square miles on USGS topo maps, and you can begin to understand why the salts have declined so precipitously on the surface of the playa. Since November 1997, however, Reilly has returned 1.9 million tons of salt onto the flats, pumping up to 7,000 gallons per minute of brine over 28,000 acres. The salt has deepened several inches since then, and the hope is that both the surface will be restored and the plant will be able to operate at a profit.

While we are standing on the berm, the sun has sunk low enough to shine in horizontally between the clouds and the mountains. The sky remains a battleship gray with tinges of pink in the distance, while the playa floor and everything on it are bathed in an intense golden light. It's like we're standing in the middle of a Misrach photo, and I urge Matt to hurry back to South Base as quickly as possible to take pictures. He demurs.

"It's cheating. It's too pretty, the light's doing all the work."

"Matt," I reply, "I'm not talking about art. I'm talking about advertising. Go get the pretty pictures so you can show them to funders, for crying out loud."

It's only with much grumbling that he concedes the point, and we race back before the light changes. When the sun gets this low, shadows can move up to fifty miles an hour across the flats. We have a window of, at most, only twenty minutes, and both of us click happily away once we're back at the Base.

I'd had a similar experience while out on the Forty Mile Desert with the Arizona photographer Mark Klett and his "Third View" team two summers previously. Finishing a day of rephotographing shots made in Nevada by Timothy O'Sullivan a hundred and twenty years earlier, we'd driven out onto the flats east of Lovelock to look for the emigrant route, which we found. Huge thunderstorms had spread over us from the west, but the sun broke through just before setting behind the mountains and washed over us in the same warm hue we were now playing in. Klett had reacted the same way as Matt, but nonetheless had taken multiple exposures that he later assembled into a striking panorama.

Today, finishing just as the sun drops into Nevada, I feel as if we've been sopping it up with the film, and am visually satiated. Matt, however, has one more treat in mind, although it's already eight o'clock. We circumnavigate the airfield, take a back road at the lower edge of town through the aluminum recycling plant with its toxic heaps of smoldering scrap, and enter the Reilly Industries property. Instead of turning left and into the plant—an antediluvian, dusty labyrinth of pipes, ducts, and conveyor belts tilted up at huge piles of salt—we turn right and drive out on a pure white road between the evaporation ponds. We don't go far.

"We have about five minutes before they come to chase us out," Matt warns as we stop. While Matt never met a No Trespassing sign he didn't like, or an open gate through which he won't drive, I'm a complete chicken and have to be dragged onto any property that's posted. But here we are, and it's worth any amount of nervousness.

We've driven out on a road of salt and, even with the sun down and the light failing, are suspended on a white line between lakes of a water the color of which I've never seen before. The closest analogy I can compare it to are those almost surreal magazine ads for Caribbean cruises, the ones that show people standing on a beach in front of a shallow tropical sea that's neither green nor blue, but a transparency in between.

The supersaturated water here is very nearly motionless, and a line of partially submerged wooden power poles marches away into the distance. The salt-laden waters glow as if reluctant to let go of the light. Rain still falls on the mountains to the south, a curtain reflected in the ponds.

"We're almost too late," apologizes Matt.

"No," I say, "this is perfect." I take two wide-angle pictures, hating the sound of the shutter.

I think about Smithson and his *Spiral Jetty,* and wonder if he should have just given up trying to make an earthwork in the salt and water and air of the lake, and come here instead. Sometimes industry just does it better. Early in his short career, and prior to meeting

Heizer, Smithson produced what he called *The Monuments of the Passaic,* an ironic guidebook to the industrial wastelands of New Jersey, and a distant progenitor of the CLUI publications like *Around Wendover* and their guide to the Test Site. He made an important point, that artists should create typologies of entropic decay in the built environment, which was as much a part of their contemporary landscape as trees and mountains. But what he missed was that sometimes the process of industry is so beautiful, even in the most classic of compositional terms or in the dramatic grammar of the romantic sublime, that it's more than ironic. It's as complicated as the balance Reilly is trying to strike between the extraction of potash and the preservation of the sodium chloride, between these dense, still waters and jet-powered cars.

The light goes and goes away until it's almost dark, and although more than fifteen minutes have passed, we've been left alone. This is the primary road for the huge dinosaurlike trucks that harvest the salts, however, and not a place to park for long, so we head back to the Unit. Ahead of us in the west, the neon of the casinos has replaced the sunset.

A Tour of the Playa   Coda: Owens Dry Lake

Ahead of us the dirt road dwindles to a strip of desiccated alkali pushed up six inches above the surface of the Owens Dry Lake. Should we fall off the track, we'll never escape from the muck that awaits on either side.

"We're heading out to the dead center of what is, on some days, the largest single point source of particulate air pollution in the United States," declares Matt, glee written all over his face. The Owens Lake is just barely dry, and only on the surface, groundwater flowing within a few feet beneath our shoes. It's not late enough in the spring for the sediments to have dried out, and we can see standing water here and there on the playa. Once again we're venturing out against better judgment, but ever since Matt made a comment on our first day in the van about Owens Lake being the anti–Los Angeles, I've had the notion we should visit it.

Fed by the watershed of the eastern Sierra Nevada, this was once a healthy perennial lake sixty miles long and 325 feet deep that had existed for 800,000 years before the drying of the climate began after the Pleistocene. Its modern travails started with agricultural withdrawals from the Owens River at the turn of the twentieth century. By 1905 the lake was only ten feet deep, but steamboats were still hauling ore across the water from the Inyo Range to the east. The lake's doom was sealed, however, when William Mulholland, an Irish ditchdigger who rose to become chief engineer and then superintendent of the Los Angeles Department of Water and Power, began excavating the Los Angeles Aqueduct in 1906 with the help of five thousand fellow pick-and-shovel enthusiasts.

With its headgates situated thirty-five miles upstream on the river, construction was finished in 1913, and the 233-mile-long straw began sucking out 27 million gallons per hour from the valley. Needless to say, not only did the complete diversion of surface water doom the lake, but the drilling of groundwater wells to augment the aqueduct's flow in drought years meant that the salt-tolerant biotic community, which was rooted in subsurface water, also died. By 1926, the lake had dried up and the surrounding area desertified into what is now more than eighty-five square miles of playa inimical to every living thing.

Residents in the small mining community located on the eastern shore of the lake have for decades complained about "Keeler fog," which the USGS notes is an "unusually fine-grained alkaline dust that infiltrates the smallest cracks and contaminates residences." The particles, which include trace minerals such as arsenic, are so fine that they are taken deep into the lungs when inhaled and cause a variety of respiratory ailments. The dust storms that rip off an average of 300,000 tons of particulates from the playa every year can be seen from satellites and are severe enough to shut down operations in the middle of the China Lake Naval Weapons Center, sixty-five miles south. Particulate emissions from the playa have been known to exceed federal health standards by as much as 2,300 percent, and the dust has settled as far away as Los Angeles and the Grand Canyon, respectively and as the crow flies (or the dust blows), 160 miles south and 320 miles east. This is America's version of the Aral Sea.

The LADWP is a founding member of the Metropolitan Water District, the MWD to which the CLUI van once belonged. Driving out onto a lake destroyed by a municipal water organization in what was once one of their sister agency's vans is guaranteed to provoke some thought.

Matt and I had discussed visiting Owens Lake while in Wendover, and after standing by the evaporation ponds there, thought it would make a nice symmetry to move from a playa where dessication was used for profit to one where it was inadvertently causing loss. Two days later, having spent a day writing up notes and exploring more of the airfield, including the *Enola Gay* hangar, we headed back south. First we retraced our way back to Tonopah, then jogged north and west over Montgomery Pass at the far end of the White Mountains, dropping into the Owens Valley to pick up my favorite road in North America, U.S. 395. Running between the 14,000-foot peaks of both the

White Mountains and the Sierra, it parallels the most continuously high mountains in the country. Two valleys to the east, Death Valley defines the other end of the spectrum. The lowest and driest real estate in North America, it's remarkably close to Mount Whitney, the highest point in the Lower 48, as well as to the Giant Sequoia groves in the southern Sierra, the largest trees on the planet and remnants of a pluvial climate.

Before visiting the lake, we stopped by the Alabama Gates, the beginning of the aqueduct that was opened early in November 1913, which were marked by a green oasis of shaded lawn surrounding a caretaker's cabin. Down the road, we swung east on state highway 136 and drove to Keeler, where the public swimming pool at the eastern edge of Owens Lake was filled with sand and abandoned travel trailers sat in a corral, mock cabañas on a toxic beach. The cause-and-effect couldn't have been more clearly polarized than by those two sites.

Keeler started out as the supply town for the Cerro Gordo silver mine high in the Inyo Mountains east of us. A steamer carried silver ingots in the early 1870s across the lake, then, later in the decade, zinc from the mine. The railroad came to town in 1883, the last of its tracks not torn out until 1960. A few dozen people remain in Keeler, but most of the residents are long gone, not just a result of the boom-and-bust of the mining but also because they couldn't handle the dust. Because the dessication of the lake has created an air pollution hazard violating EPA standards, the City of Los Angeles and its Metropolitan Water District are now required to mitigate the blowing dust. Tackling a few square miles each year since 1999, they are returning 40,000 acre-feet of flow to the playa every year (about enough water for 200,000 people in the city). They're also replanting native vegetation and covering portions of the lake bed with gravel, the work to be finished by 2005.

The fugitive dust blowing off the playa has been studied extensively since the 1980s by several agencies, including China Lake, the

Swimming pool in Keeler, Nevada. CLUI Archive

EPA, and the USGS. The only recent construction in town was an encampment belonging to the Desert Research Institute (DRI) from Nevada, which is under contract to measure air quality, and which, judging from the number of trucks and equipment parked next to its cluster of single-wide units, was keeping busy. It was almost six o'clock when we arrived in Keeler, too late in the day to find anyone to interview, so Matt turned the van out onto the playa.

Despite the fact that what passes for a road isn't elevated much above the treacherous alkaline mud around us, its single-lane width is surprisingly well packed and firm, and we soon see why. Heavy equipment is parked on subsidiary jetties of dirt, pits and trenches being dug everywhere as part of the mitigation work. We follow one of the spurs north, Matt looking for a CLUI art project placed here in 1996. We find it, a forlorn pole barely visible out in the playa, but we have to scramble down into and out of one of the trenches that's between the road and the piece. Luckily, this part of the lake bed has already dried out to some degree. The surface is desiccating like crumpled paper, not yet sanded down by wind to a smooth finish, an effect Matt hasn't seen before, a result of the groundwater percolating up through capillary action and producing what's called "self-rising" or "puffy" ground.

The structure of the CLUI is flexible enough to embrace both documentarians such as Matt and a roving group of anonymous artists and engineers who install subversive commentaries, such as Kunkle's camera obscuras on bombing ranges, and in 1995 a working water-cooler in the middle of the Algodones Dunes, a heavily overused recreational area in Southern California—and this piece, a solar-powered tape recorder that at night plays the sounds of lapping water where no one will hear it, where there's no water to lap, and where even the nearby work crews won't notice it. Begging the question of whether or not waves exist if there's no one to hear them, the tape loop is more an object to be written about than to be witnessed, following

Wassergeist **sound-emitting device on Owens Dry Lake, California.** CLUI Archive

Working water-cooler in Algodones Dunes, California. CLUI Archive

the precedent of earthworks, which are seen more often in photographs than visited.

We troop out to the pole, and Matt examines the recorder and solar cells, the latter splattered with bird shit. The sound sculpture was placed here in 1995, and he hasn't been able to visit it since last year. Usually the recorder emits a small hum, but apparently it's no longer working.

"The engineering on this was really crude," he says, shaking his head. "We had to invent it all, but now it's off-the-shelf and we could do a better job." He's thinking about the solar-powered installations that we're seeing during this trip, from the self-contained, radar-emitting "threats" captured from foreign militaries and then placed by the air force in remote desert locations, part of our electronic warfare ranges, to the DRI's sophisticated air-monitoring rigs out here on the playa.

While Matt takes pictures, recording the current status of the device and its surroundings from every angle, I walk away a few paces. Within only yards I can no longer hear the clicking of Matt's camera, but the silence is disrupted by a pair of F-something-or-other fighter-bombers returning from their last flight of the day. They're headed north, perhaps to the Fallon Naval Air Station. Although several hundred miles away, it's a short flight for the jets, which roam across the western United States in Military Operation Areas that extend almost unbroken from Mexico to Canada, air corridors that the armed services are always lobbying to increase. Air space in the country is already so restricted by the military that commercial airlines now have trouble routing passenger traffic, a conflict that will only grow more strident as we build faster weapons requiring larger spaces in which to train pilots. This is one of the reasons the air force is testing unmanned aircraft (UAVs) at Nellis. Not only does their use decrease the political fallout from pilots being shot down, but the UAVs are much smaller, infinitely more maneuverable, and don't need expansive (and expensive) training.

Once the jets have disappeared over the horizon, which takes only a few seconds, I'm left with more personal thoughts. I've been driving by this playa for thirty-four years, and once ventured down the road leading to an industrial compound on its western shore. It was late on a January day in, I think, the late 1960s, and the playa was covered with water, sky and ephemeral lake the same shade of winter-gray. I thought then it was one of the most mysterious places I'd ever been, and still think so. I didn't know it then, but Owens Lake generates some of the most salt-laden dust in the country, and as a result sends up to one hundred times more dust aloft than other playas. It's an artificial dead sea when wet, and when dry a vast junkyard of rusting metal. Old mining equipment, boat parts and anchors, auto bodies . . . the flotsam of mechanized civilization is scattered across the flat, slowly sinking into the sediments in the dry-wet-dry cycle of the playa. Smithson would have enjoyed it here.

Driving out across the playas of Nevada and Utah since I was sixteen apparently has made a deep impression in my mind; ever since my early twenties, I've had recurring dreams of traveling on a desert road that disappears underneath flood waters. Sometimes I'm able to push carefully through on the invisible road, but usually not, and I've always wondered what the connection might be between playas and the state of my life, metaphorical or real.

When Matt's finished, we trudge back to the van and spend the next hour wandering around the playa, following roads to a variety of mitigation efforts, hopeful that we can find a way clear across the dry lake and back to U.S. 395. At times we're driving with water on both sides of us, and in the gathering dusk it's all too eerily like my dream.

There's one site where we have to stop and take a picture, though. A black woven-plastic mesh runs out several hundred yards to the east. What's normally a snow fence used by highway crews to prevent drifts from burying roads apparently has been deployed here in an attempt to stop the migrating dust. Within a few yards, the fence dives downward into the alkali and salt. Perhaps it's achieving its purpose, but it looks more like an experiment overcome by earth, air, and water, logic submerged in the surreal. Not far away is a solar-powered telemetry device, either a dust trap or a particle counter. The playa here looks like nothing else so much as Frenchman Flat, industrial detritus interspersed with monitoring instruments. It's a plain of man-made devastation being probed for cost-effective environmental mitigation no less than its nuclear cousin to the east.

Our quest for a passage is increasingly slowed by soft spots in the road that are becoming deeper and longer. Plus, the sun has now dipped below Mount Whitney to the west. Trying to stay on the roads in the dark wouldn't be fun, so it's time to leave. We keep driving down the track looking for a place to turn around, Matt getting out to check the depth of the dust. One patch is just too extensive to risk crossing, and Matt reluctantly puts the van in reverse, driving backward for some minutes before finding a junction where we can make the maneuver. We reach Keeler and the paved surface of Highway 136 at 7:05 P.M. just as the shadow of the Sierra hits the eastern side of the valley.

We're not a minute too soon. Now that we've stopped and rolled down the windows, safe from the dust, I can hear a tire losing air at a rapid rate. It's on the rear passenger side, and we set to changing it. Loosening the lug nuts, I find they're so hot I can't touch them; the other wheels are equally overheated, something I've never seen before. Plus, there's no discernible puncture in the tire, which was leaking air so fast we saw it flattening when we got out. Our only guess is that we've accumulated enough alkali dust underneath the van to create friction somewhere for the wheels. That may or may not account for the flat tire, but it at least explains the heat, one of those haphazard theories with little reason behind it that serve to calm the nerves in the desert. Almost any explanation will suffice to reassure travelers when faced with chaos in the Big Empty, yet another cognitive coping mechanism.

It's dark by the time we're back on 395. We skip dinner and head south for home. At nine o'clock a severe crosswind in Antelope Valley tears off half of the plywood platform atop the van and sends it cartwheeling into the median. Fortunately, there's no one immediately behind us, and Matt pulls over, climbs up on top, and, despite what we later learn were sixty-miles-per-hour gusts, manages to rip off the remaining sheet of wood, which was threatening to pull apart the roof.

Minus half an exhaust system, a tire, and the photo rig, we reach my place just before eleven. We've driven more than two thousand miles, seen twenty-three separate playas, and only managed to increase our appetite for more. Matt travels to Germany in two weeks to see how the dead factories of the Rühr Valley are being transformed—a possible source of ideas for Wendover—while I have to return to Las Vegas to write an article on a multi-billion-dollar luxury real-estate development being built around the largest privately owned artificial lake in Nevada, capitalism birthing yet another anti-playa.

Painting the Playa   Smoke Creek Desert

Michael Moore, a tall, genial artist in his mid-fifties from the San Francisco Bay Area, is sitting on a seat hacked out of an enormous white tree trunk that's beached on its side at the edge of the Smoke Creek playa in Northern Nevada. Linda Fleming, a sculptor and Mike's wife, has created several works here, this vantage point among them. Mike and others helped drag "The Behemoth," as they refer to the poplar-tree trunk, out here to the edge of the sands, where she cleaned it off and transformed it into a sitting sculpture. Behind us, the truncated remains of the root system reach out like a giant maw seeking to devour the view westward. This late May afternoon, Mike and I are perched on the more friendly end, watching a dust storm blow itself out on the eastern side of the playa. Dark storm clouds had followed me this morning as I drove the 120 miles north from Reno and across the narrow neck of alkali flats that connect the Black Rock and Smoke Creek deserts. Rain is a promise made and broken here more often than not, today being no exception, although the mountains to the south by Pyramid Lake are obscured now by what might be a thunderstorm. With the wind coming up this hard from the south, it's impossible to separate rain from blowing dust at a distance.

Mike and Linda are just finishing an expansion to their house, sitting about a quarter of a mile behind us, which will bring up their desert retreat from city life to around 1,200 square feet of living space, not counting Linda's separate 24-foot-by-24-foot sculpture studio. They aren't the first artists to settle here, but the most recent. To my left and north are the trees that mark the springs at the end of the playa where another California escapee, John Bogard, established the Planet X pottery in 1974, making functional crockery that often depicts the playa on its surfaces. Understanding how Moore's playa paintings fit into the art history of the region requires some digressions.

The Black Rock, along with what's sometimes considered its sister lobe, the Smoke Creek, have been legendary playas virtually since Frémont crossed the region in January 1844. Some emigrants chose to cross the Black Rock instead of the Forty Mile Desert to the southeast, thinking the northern course would be a more-watered route. They were misled. Others were diverted from the main trail by Oregonians hoping they would take the Applegate-Lassen Cutoff to settle in that state instead of California—a trend that people in Portland now wish had never been started. But the Black Rock was, along with the western part of the Great Salt Lake Desert and the Forty Mile Desert, one of the most barren and waterless parts of the entire route; its cultural status was gained at first through misery, and only later through beauty.

J. Goldsborough Bruff (1804–1889), a forty-five-year-old former draftsman for the U.S. Bureau of Topographical Engineers, left us a thorough record of the journey. The son of a physician and surrounded by family members who were engineers and artists, Bruff was apparently a bit of a strong-willed misfit. Allowed to resign from West Point when he was sixteen for fighting a duel, he went to sea, and by 1827 he was a naval draftsman responsible for drawing the complicated rigging of large ships as well as coastal fortifications and maps. He later designed much of the ornamental work for the U.S. Treasury Building, and in 1846 he drew the first official map of Florida as a state.

Bruff was bitten by the gold bug in early 1849 and decided to light out for the California hills. He thought he might put his topographical skills to use, so, in addition to forming the Washington City and California Mining Association—a company of sixty-four men to head West—he decided he would keep a detailed and illustrated journal of the trip and afterward publish a guidebook to the trail. The group left Washington in April 1849; when entering the Black Rock on September 21st of that year, which Bruff said "looks like a plain of ice," he reported seeing a standing mirage of "a long lagoon of light blue water" that appeared to be bordered by tall trees. It was such a compelling sight that "oxen had stampeded for it, hoping to quench their burning thirst, and left their swelled up carcasses over the plain in that direction, as far as we could discern them." He counted the carcasses of 103 dead oxen, 36 horses, and 1 mule at Rabbit Hole Springs—and that was just at the entrance to the Black Rock Desert; 50 more dead oxen awaited him at Black Rock Springs, which sits at the fork of the western and eastern arms of the playa. His sketch of the carnage surrounding Rabbit Hole became a well-known early image of death by thirst during the Gold Rush.

Some people still have a morbid fascination with a place that's so dangerous in legend and fact, which helps explain part of the popularity of the Burning Man Festival that takes place on that playa every Labor Day Weekend, and an event I'll attend later this summer. But others have been drawn to it by images made later of its encompassing starkness, the visual quality of which falls into that category of scenery we label sublime: places where nature is overwhelmingly present, beyond obvious human intervention, and capable of killing you. The unstable glaciers and avalanche-prone faces of the Swiss Alps are good examples, that mountain range being the prototypical sublime landscape for European art audiences in the eighteenth and nineteenth centuries, a scenery of literally high drama represented in popular paintings by artists such as J. M. W. Turner and, in turn, the bedrock upon which artists such as Bierstadt and Moran would erect their sometimes portentous revisions of the mountains and chasms of the American West. The perception of American deserts in general, and of the playas in particular, however, would be grafted onto traditional European schemes for the sublime and the exotic only with some effort.

When Frémont noted that the Great Basin elicited comparisons with Asiatic scenery, he wasn't simply making a statement of geological fact but an aesthetic and political appeal to his readers' imaginations (and hence to his superiors, such as his father-in-law, the influential expansionist U.S. Senator Thomas Hart Benton). Egypt, the Holy Land, and Asia were seen as lands of mystery, a widespread public perception created by the reports from a relatively new discipline, archaeology, and from pictures of ancient ruins being disseminated through lithographs by traveling artists such as the Englishman David

Roberts. Pictures of these wondrous antiquities were being published in America during the same decade that Frémont was exploring the Great Basin, and were as popular on the East Coast as on the Continent.

The American deserts didn't have crumbling ruins to match the Near and Far East, but they had a magnificent geology wherein the passage of time was uniquely visible, the science of the planet laid bare. Frémont deliberately conflated the American and Near Eastern deserts when naming the first body of water he found after exiting the Smoke Creek Valley. Tagging Pyramid Lake for its most visible shoreline feature, he explicitly compared it with the pyramids of Cheops in his published description. When Clarence King came through Nevada twenty years after Frémont with the photographer Timothy O'Sullivan, he again made the connection when he renamed a formation of columnar rhyolite above Lovelock, which previously had been known as Crab's Claw Peak. Again Egypt was evoked, and he anointed it "Karnak Ridge" after the largest collection of ruins in that country.

Just as the British Empire had established a pictorial hegemony over its territories, in part to encourage commerce, immigration, and tourism, so did the American government use visual means to do the same in North America. In order to more firmly link the West, and most importantly California, with the eastern half of the country, the federal government sponsored surveying expeditions from 1838 through the Pacific railroad surveys of the 1850s. Spending up to a third of the national budget annually on the expeditions and their subsequent publications, with the printing of the heavily illustrated volumes sometimes costing up to three times the costs of the actual expeditions, the government distributed hundreds of thousands of copies to the public. According to Ron Tyler's study of government prints at the Library of Congress, *Prints of the West*, several artists contributed more than seven hundred drawings and paintings to the railroad reports alone. Unfortunately, the playas are sorely underrepresented.

Charles Preuss, besides serving as Frémont's cartographer, also made sketches of the terrain they traversed, including the first picture of Pyramid Lake. He apparently did not find anything remarkable to record on the Black Rock or the Smoke Creek playas. Stansbury's 1849 journey to survey a possible route for the railroad from Missouri to the Great Salt Lake was another official expedition. As was customary, an artist accompanied him, Franklin R. Grist, who by February 1850 was replaced by a young English traveler, John Hudson. Although the expedition produced numerous and wondrous views of the lake, its islands, and the surrounding mountains, and a panoramic view from Bear River Bay, apparently neither artist made views of the flats themselves, perhaps partially a reflection of their leader's disgust with their endless mud and drudgery.

The problem early artists had with the playas is that most of them were unable to perceive any "there" there. In 1867, the photographer Charles R. Savage complained that, once you were past the Wasatch Range outside Salt Lake City, there were few features that could be combined to make a decent picture, and that the farther west one went, the more uninteresting it became until it was, simply, desert. The major artistic exception may be in one of the four panoramas made by Friedrich W. von Egloffstein, a Prussian-born artist, engineer, and writer.

Egloffstein was a master topographer who would eventually go on to invent a shading technique for depicting landforms, an important precursor to both contour mapping and the halftone process by which most photographs are printed in books. He engraved exquisitely and with precision the maps drawn by Preuss and Frémont, and in 1857 himself drew a signature image of the Grand Canyon, *Big Cañon at Mouth of Diamond River,* an exaggerated and gothic depiction that makes the chasm appear as if it had been created by that master of the romantic horrorscape, Gustave Doré.

The four panoramas made earlier by Egloffstein during Lieutenant Beckwith's 1854 survey of the 38th parallel—the survey that explored what would become eventually the central railroad route—are foldouts that each cover from seventy to a hundred miles of the horizon in a single extremely accurate sweep. Egloffstein met Beckwith's party in Salt Lake City in mid-1854, after the survey's original leader, Gunnison, who had served with Stansbury on the Salt Lake Survey, was killed during an Indian attack, the only such incident during the railroad surveys. Command of the party was given to Beckwith, Gunnison's second-in-command, who promptly set about preparations to continue the work westward.

Egloffstein's panoramas trace their journey past Pilot Peak and over into the Humboldt Range, across the Black Rock and into the northern Sierra, where the surveyors ended their work in the Sacramento River Valley. The depictions he made later of the Grand Canyon were cast in an increasingly romantic manner, but these works are relatively straightforward, very much in the tradition of topographical illustration practiced by explorers the world over. *Valley of the Mud Lakes,* the lithograph included in the published reports, was made by C. Shumann from Egloffstein's drawings and verified against the original cartography done by Preuss when he passed through with Frémont. The "mud lakes" are, in fact, the Smoke Creek and Black Rock playas. As mentioned in the introduction, the panorama covers more than eighty miles from end to end, and 7,200 square miles of topography. The central fact of this picture are the playas, the mountains serving only to delineate the geographically enclosed basins. It was a treatment chosen not so much out of aesthetic concerns but necessitated by the engineering requirements of the survey, exactly the sort of quantitative constraints that would produce the next stage of playa works. If Egloffstein had to illustrate the dead-level playa grades the railroad companies could use to their advantage, so science would apply a precision pictorialism in order to understand their origin.

In 1874 a young geologist, Israel Cook Russell (1852–1906), talked his way into the U.S. Naval Observatory's Transit of Venus Expedition to New Zealand and Kerguelen Island. Russell, just two years out of the University of New York with a degree in civil engineering, was so

Detail from Frederick W. von Egloffstein, "Valley of the Mud Lakes." This panorama appears in *Reports of Exploration and Surveys to Ascertain the Most Practicable and Economical Route for a Railroad from the Mississippi River to the Pacific Ocean*, Vol. 11 (Washington, D.C., 1861). Reproduced with the permission of Alvin McLane keen to go that even though there was no position for a geologist, he signed on as the expedition photographer, learning how to operate a camera before leaving. Kerguelen Island is one of the more austere locations in the world. Located on the edge of the Antarctic Convergence, where the Antarctic Ocean meets the Pacific, and about halfway between Africa and Australia, it was first discovered in 1772. When Captain James Cook sailed to it two years later, he called the grim volcanic outcropping the Island of Desolation. Its dark cliffs catch the storms where two great weather systems collide, producing one of the most miserable climates imaginable three hundred days out of the year. Russell and the crew spent three months there, obtaining the first observed transit of Venus since Cook had successfully viewed it in the previous century.

Apparently Russell found hardship outdoors to his liking, because he became a renowned expert on much of the western states and provinces of North America, surveying desert lakes from below sea level to mountain glaciers above 10,000 feet. Just under medium height and of slight build, the taciturn young man hardly looked the part of an intrepid explorer, but he served with the USGS from 1880 through 1892, and in 1888 he helped found the National Geographic Society, an organization for which he led an expedition to Alaska's Mount Saint Elias in order to survey it. In 1896 he mapped Mount Rainer, and in 1901 the Craters of the Moon in Idaho. But Russell had first established his bona fides in the Great Basin, starting in 1881 with a seven-month solo reconnaissance of the area once covered by the ancient Lake Lahontan. Covering 3,500 miles alone on horseback that first field season didn't seem to bother him; on the contrary, judging from the language in his subsequent reports, I would submit that it made him the first poet of the region.

He returned a second year with a small survey party, conducted a full season's work based out of Winnemucca, then wintered over in Salt Lake City into spring 1883. By July of that third summer, he was ready to start north from the Mono Basin to recheck his observations and work up again through the Black Rock and Smoke Creek deserts and into Red Bluff, California, where he finally disbanded his party in October. They had surveyed 90,000 square miles, established the nature, duration, and extent of the Pleistocene Lake Lahontan, and completed the fieldwork for what would be the benchmark study of the Lake Lahontan portion of the Great Basin. Anyone wishing to write about Nevada, whether it's to describe the geology or its art, which are often inseparable, would do well to start with Russell's 1885 report, *Geological History of Lake Lahontan: A Quaternary Lake of Northwestern Nevada.*

Russell begins his study by echoing Frémont, but he quickly becomes more specific, saying that travelers must compare the region to the deserts of Arabia and to the shores of the Dead Sea. He notes how the playas in summer become "so sun-cracked as to resemble tessellated pavements of cream-colored marble," how the salts effloresce like "drifting snow," and how dust devils, "swinging and bending columns," rise up two thousand feet like "pillars of smoke." He writes of "aeolian sands" occupying a belt of desert floor forty miles long and ten wide, where seventy-five-foot-thick drifts have buried telegraph poles so deeply that new poles had to be spliced atop them to keep the wires above the crests of the dunes. His language utilizes images that readers could compare with their own surroundings and that enable them to imagine the landforms as ruined monuments.

He notes that the Great Salt Lake will bring to mind familiar descriptions of the Dead Sea in Palestine, and acknowledges that to the American artist the scenery of the humid regions is in sharp contrast with the Great Basin, with its "russet-brown desolation of the valleys, the brilliant colors of the naked rocks, and the sharp angular outlines of the mountains." Russell even gives cognitive clues to the uneasiness suffered by the playa traveler in a passage that describes the visual dissonance of the playas: "When the sun is high in the cloudless heavens and one is far out on the desert at a distance from rocks and trees, there is a lack of shadow and an absence of relief in the landscape that

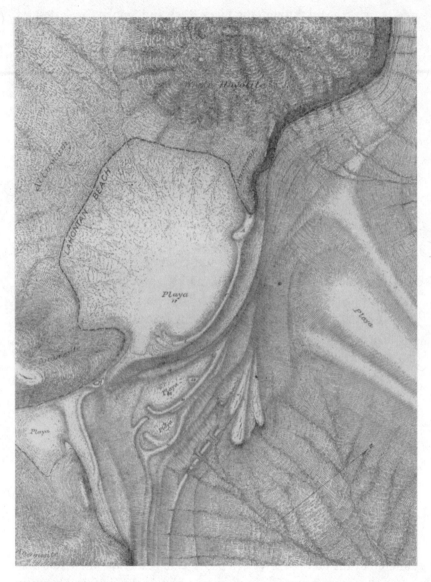

"Gravel Embankments on South Border of the Carson Desert, Nevada." I. C. Russell, geologist; W. D. Johnson, topographer. This image appears in *Geological History of Lake Lahontan: A Quaternary Lake of Northwestern Nevada* (Washington, D.C.: United States Geological Survey, 1885). Reproduced with the permission of Alvin McLane make the distance deceptive—the mountains appearing near at hand instead of leagues away—and cause one to fancy that there is no single source of light, but that the distant ranges and the desert surfaces are self-luminous."

His report included maps, topographical sketches, extensive cross-sections of the geology, and aerial views. The latter were constructed remarkably from nothing but knowledge gained on the ground, and they represent sea cliffs, barrier bars, embankments, deltas, and terraces both built and cut from cliffs by the wave action of the ancient waters. Four artists and cartographers accompanied him: George Wright, W. J. McGee, A. L. Webster, and Willard D. Johnson. Wright and McGee were his "geological aides," with McGee drawing up to six geological sections on double page foldouts reminiscent of those by the greatest of all American topographical artists, the incomparable William Holmes, who worked on the Dutton survey of the Grand Canyon a decade earlier. Webster, assisted by a crew member named Eugene Ricksecker, did the pocket map for the published report, as well as the small illustrations, while Johnson did the hatched topo maps, borrowing his technique from Egloffstein.

Although Mono Lake lies outside the Lahontan Basin, it too is a relict body of water, and a separate account by Russell of his work there was published in the *Eighth Annual Report* of the usgs in 1889. The Lahontan book is currently out of print, but the Mono Lake report has been reprinted and is one of the more readily available examples of late-nineteenth-century visual representation of the West, featuring the cartographic work of Johnson and others.

Russell's reports became a model for the scientists of the usgs and elsewhere for diligence and detail in field observations. He maintained a lifelong enthusiasm for the arid lands of the desert Southwest, quick to point out that the lack of vegetation made readily visible the features of the land, and that his experiences there led to creating the field of physiography itself, a descriptive system that geologists now refer to as geomorphology.

Other images of playas were made by scientists and travelers at the end of the nineteenth and beginning of the twentieth centuries, but they're often buried in government records. The USGS retains some of the pictures, one being the photograph "Clayton Valley Salt Flat, from Mineral Ridge, near Silver Peak, Esmeralda County, Nevada," taken in 1896 by the third director of the agency, C. D. Walcott. Another, "Lake Bonneville shoreline on east wall of Cache Valley, Logan Quadrangle, Cache County, Utah" from around 1901, was taken by Russell's boss at the USGS, G. K. Gilbert. Called the greatest geomorphologist in the history of science, Gilbert was the person who studied the faulting of the West and named the twenty-million-year-old province "Basin-Range" for its four hundred mountain blocks that had rotated up from the horizontal. Surveying the shorelines of the ancient Lake Bonneville at the same time Russell was laboriously tracing Lahontan, Gilbert, too, displayed an appreciation for the playas, although, as the title of his photo demonstrates, not as poetic an imagination.

Nonetheless, the views in the USGS photos by Walcott and Gilbert are deliberately framed, the scientists careful to include mountains for scale and drama as well as geological context. I take pains to list the names of these geologists and their cartographers because they, along with Timothy O'Sullivan, T. H. Watkins, and the other photographers who soon followed to picture the region for science and commerce, built the framework around which other artists have constructed their visions of the desert. A prime example is Maynard Dixon (1875–1946), who painted the mountains and playas of Nevada throughout much of his life.

Mike and I are starting to suffer from sore butts, sitting on the immense poplar trunk and watching the dust blow by, so we start back toward the house. Despite the airborne alkali out on the playa, our feet sink into the ground. It's wetter here at the edge of the Smoke Creek playa than it was on Owens Lake a month earlier, when Matt Coolidge and I were out trooping around, in part because I'm now three hundred miles to the north and more than three thousand feet higher in elevation. Spring hasn't yet advanced as far here.

Mike and Linda were married on the Smoke Creek in January 1996. Since then, they've built the house, drilled a well, and created a modest riparian environment with five interconnected ponds that now host coots, ducks, and herons, a variety of fish, and bullfrogs that sing most of the night. They've planted 120 trees and reseeded the disturbed desert soils with native grasses, such as wild rye, which is punctuated with scarlet paintbrush blooming beside clumps of yellow rabbit brush. As we come up off the clay of the playa and onto firmer soil, underfoot is an intermittent but impressive lithic scatter of worked stone, the flakes from obsidian and chert points indicating the extensive hunting that once occurred here.

A larger, two-story house sits next to the springs at the old Parker Ranch, a quarter-mile south of Mike and Linda's place. It's a handsome square structure surrounded by porches that Mike designed for their close friend, the art and map collector David Rumsey. Among the three of them, they own 480 acres in the valley, most of it covered by three kinds of sagebrush and cheatgrass. As we swing up past David's place, the local herd of wild horses circles out ahead, four adults and three colts. The stallion brings up the rear, keeping an eye on us. To the west are the Buffalo Hills, a steep escarpment of dark-red Tertiary lava. In the canyons carved into the tablelands up above, the hills become a convoluted landscape in which hundreds of wild horses hide so successfully that the BLM doesn't even bother to send its helicopters there for periodic roundups.

These are the hills that Mike looked out at from the trailer they brought up here while they were building the house, a range to which he's become very attached. He regularly walks up through breaks in the cliffs, checks on them all the time while we're down here, broods on them. They remind me of the hills in Maynard Dixon's paintings of Nevada, a not-unnatural association, since Mike had the artist in mind when looking for a place in Nevada to build a studio.

In fact, he had a specific painting as a role model—*Home of the Desert Rat,* a Utah scene that Dixon painted in 1945, the year before he died. A mountain dominates the right-hand side of the picture, and shadows sweep in from the left side of the canvas, accentuating the horizontals of a *bajada,* or aggregate of alluvial fans, at the foot of which is perched a small shack next to a clutch of trees. The brush-work is loose and confident, the outlines of the land sharp in the desert air. The shadows have overtaken the house, and the strong triangles of the mountains will soon retreat into darkness. It's a lonely, peaceful picture and represents the solitude to which Dixon was drawn his entire life.

Born in Fresno in 1875, Dixon was an asthmatic child who started drawing when he was seven years old. His grandfather, who had a ranch in the San Joaquin Valley, was also an amateur draftsman, and Dixon was encouraged to sketch the long horizons and open spaces of his childhood. By the time he was sixteen, he had quit school and started to study art on his own, going so far as to send his idol, the western artist Frederic Remington, two of his notebooks. Remington wrote back with encouragement. When Dixon's mother moved to the Bay Area in 1893, he tried attending the San Francisco Institute of Design, but after only three months he left school again and began doing magazine illustrations for the local *Overland Monthly.* Dixon would continue to do magazine work until 1912, publishing more than two hundred illustrations in regional and national periodicals such as *Sunset, Scribners,* and *Harpers Weekly.*

In 1899, the artist went to work for the *San Francisco Examiner,* but by the next year he had found the atmosphere too nerve-wracking, and he began to travel extensively throughout the desert Southwest while maintaining a studio in the city, a practice upon which he would play variations until he died. He did studies of the mining camps in Goldfield and Tonopah, sketched among the Navajo and Hopi tribes, and visited Mexico. In 1906, the San Francisco Earthquake destroyed his studio and everything in it, except for a few drawings and Navajo blankets. He and his wife took the loss of possessions as an opportunity to move to New York, where they stayed until 1912. It was a productive time for Dixon, and their social circle included Charles Russell and Will James as frequent visitors, among whose company he was now accepted as an equal. But with his exposure to the avant-garde, which was being imported to America from Europe by people such as the gallery owner and photographer Alfred Stieglitz, this sojourn would also provide a platform from which Dixon could later depart the mainstream of American realism and narrative art.

Upon return to the West, Dixon was offered a substantial commission to do a four-part mural based on Indian themes for a mansion near Pasadena. The results were so satisfactory that murals became an important source of revenue for him, and he completed eighteen of them, the last one from his deathbed. They were a welcome relief from the cowboy-and-Indian stereotypes that magazine editors were constantly demanding but not yet enough to support him when he and his wife divorced in mid-decade. Dixon went to work for an advertising company, accepted miscellaneous painting commissions, and even tried teaching, but he was no better at that than he had been as a student. In 1919, following some time off recuperating from a crippling bout of rheumatism, he escaped to Carson City, Nevada, to sketch. When he returned to San Francisco, he met the young photographer Dorothea Lange. They were married in March 1920.

And here it's worth taking a breath, because this is when Dixon's work makes a remarkable jump that lifts him out of the ranks of the illustrators and regional artists, and provides him with a niche all his own in the country's history of art. Studying the night sky at his Russian Hill home one evening and examining the clouds, Dixon apparently had an epiphany: by simplifying the compositional elements of his paintings into dominate patterns and lines, he would greatly increase the psychological and spiritual impact of the work. An example I favor is the 34-inch-by-62-inch oil, *Cloud World*.

Anyone familiar with the work of Georgia O'Keeffe (1887–1986), whom Dixon met in 1923, knows her immense 1965 painting *Sky Above Clouds IV.* She painted the 8-foot-by-24-foot canvas, a skyscape seen from above and filled to the horizon with oval clouds, after taking an airplane trip back to New Mexico. It's a glorious painting, more subtle than it appears at first glance, and one that took an enormous physical effort for the seventy-eight-year-old painter to construct, much less prepare for transport to exhibition. It has metaphorical, if not stylistic, links to Agnes Martin's desert minimalism, organizing into a meditative state that largest of terrestrial spaces, the sky, through the sheer force of pattern. But Dixon had prefigured that painting by forty years.

In Dixon's 1925 *Cloud World,* the clouds are seen from below, to be sure, but in their checkerboard regularity (and their upper oval shapes, implicit from this low angle), and even in the horizontal bands of red mesas and dark foreground, the two paintings echo each other strongly. When in New York City, Dixon had found Stieglitz a disagreeable and exploitive person, but he and O'Keeffe in the 1920s were on something of the same wavelength, both of them reducing their western landscapes down to intensified geometries that had a sharpness of line and lack of clutter in common with work by the Precisionist painters Charles Demuth and Charles Sheeler. The two cloud paintings by Dixon and O'Keeffe were done four decades apart, but looking at the work of these two artists from the 1920s, it's clear they were both influenced by European abstraction, yet making something very American out of it.

Dixon had been showing his work since 1916 with artists such as John Marin, Stuart Davis, Sheeler, Demuth, and even Picasso and Matisse. He was not only aware of the European and American avant-garde traditions but actively promoted exhibitions of them in San Francisco. He might have held up Remington and the other great illustrators of the late nineteenth century, such as N. C. Wyeth, as his heroes and peers while early in his career, but in 1912 he had declared himself an illustrator no more. He was an artist.

Dixon himself never became an avant-gardist in his temperament or his work, and he pretty much hewed to "the evidence in front of his eyes," or so he claimed in the last catalog statement he made before he passed away. But he borrowed freely from whomever he needed to in order to develop an original style—as an artist now, not an illustrator—that would present that evidence in a manner allowing it a measure of mythology beyond the confines of pure representation. What challenged artists painting the arid West, avant-garde or not, wasn't just the art history of Europe but the cognitive dissonance they suffered in the Big Empty—not only were they burdened with navigating their way around the deserts of the Southwest, but they had to find new ways to represent them in original spatial hierarchies.

For Dixon this came, albeit slowly, in the form of what he called "cubist realism," where he reduced individual landscape elements into pattern. By the early 1920s, cubism, the twentieth century's first great experimental art movement, had thoroughly infiltrated the art circles of New York, where it was taken by avant-garde artists as the basis for a geometrical organization of the visual world. For Dixon, this meant a somewhat realistic, if graphic, treatment of the foreground, a tendency to distill landforms into large structural blocks, and the organization of the background into geometry. In the cloud paintings from 1925, for example, it's the atmosphere he was dicing up into squares. If the cubism of Paris and Braque and Picasso had been shaped by the influx of African art, Dixon's was molded by the Late Classic Period weavings of the Navajo, and the "eyedazzler" rugs of which he was so fond—the patterns of the American Indians being yet another example of how to organize the large spaces of the desert into visually consistent and navigable geometrics.

Dixon had never really painted the landscape the way Bierstadt and Moran had. Coming out of the literally more-humid atmosphere of the Hudson River School and European landscape traditions, those two men would fill their paintings with detail and progressively soften the contours of the land in order to indicate distance. Dixon kept making his paintings simpler, losing details in order to pick up the fundamental shapes of landforms. The ridges on even his most-distant mountains and mesas retain their clarity of edge, a stylistic convention that matched the arid reality of the southwestern air but was also well suited to the graphic and mural work he was commissioned to do. It was an aesthetic choice the earlier topographic artists would have recognized, yet one that also flowed from Whistler's dictum that the artist is known for what he omits.

From the mid-1920s onward, Dixon's paintings tend to be organized around long horizontals in the land and sky. His brushwork is looser and more confident, even as the compositions become more delineated. That decade saw his mural work flourish, a business that dropped off only when the Great Depression arrived in late 1929 and businesses no longer had discretionary income to spend on art. In 1930, he and Dorothea bought a Model-T Ford and drove to Taos, where they lived among the denizens of its art colony. By 1934 he was working at Hoover Dam to document the construction, one of the artists hired by the federal government's labor program, the Public Works of Art Project.

By 1935 Dixon's home life was once again falling apart; at sixty years of age, he was divorced from Lange, and it was evident that the chronic asthma he had suffered since his boyhood, a condition aggravated by his fondness for hand-rolled cigarettes, had developed into severe emphysema. Two years later, he remarried, this time to the young San Francisco muralist Edith Hamlin. Late in the decade, his lungs growing steadily worse, they moved to Tucson where they stayed during the winters, spending summers at a retreat they had built near Zion National Park. Dixon died in 1945, the year he painted *Home of the Desert Rat,* a picture that would, among other things, inspire Mike Moore to find a studio in Nevada.

Dixon left behind almost eight hundred oil paintings, having had more than thirty one-person exhibitions during his lifetime and work in hundreds of group shows. He had traveled on horseback throughout the playas of Nevada and California, painting the Black Rock Desert, Death Valley, the increasingly desiccated Owens Lake, and the alkaline beds of the Carson Sink. Following Israel C. Russell, and prior to the widespread coming of the automobile, he probably covered as much of the territory as any other artist of his time and began the process of broadening its visual representation from the literal to the metaphorical.

Dixon left us some paintings that we now tend to put in the art history bin as pleasantly pictorial, and some that verge on being more merely graphic than artistic—but he also created landscapes that remain definitive tropes for how we perceive the mountains and playas of the West. By painting the desert as architectonic shapes composed of monochromatic planes, he illuminated not only the structural geology of the region but the very ways in which our cognitive neurophysiology seeks to reduce visual input through hardwired rules of boundary recognition and contrast.

A much-less-known artist in what would become a growing tradition of landscape abstraction was Robert Caples (1908–1979). Raised in New York City, and like Dixon a restless and sickly child, he studied briefly at both the National Academy of Design and the Art Student's League before being sent in 1924, when he was sixteen, to live with his father in Reno. After a stay at the Community Arts School in Santa Barbara, he returned to Reno in 1928 and set up a portrait studio, becoming part of an arts scene that, as Mike reminds me, was the basis for Walter Van Tilburg Clark's novel, *The City of Trembling Leaves*.

Caples maintained this eminently social practice until 1932, when, becoming disgusted with the vainglorious demands of his clients, he gathered up all his sketches and works-in-progress, tore them into quarters, and dumped them in an alleyway trash can. During the Depression, and again like Dixon, he found work with various government art projects, notably working on the murals in San Francisco's Coit Tower, where he may very well have met the older man. He found time to study etching, printmaking, and painting with several regional artists during the 1930s, in particular mentioning later to his novelist friend Clark that he was intrigued by the "oriental simplicity" of Bill Gaskin's work.

World War II found Caples in the Caribbean slathering gray paint on ship hulls with a six-inch-wide brush for the U.S. Navy, at least until his Indian sketches were noticed by an admiral's wife and he was transferred to the Hydrographic Bureau to draw maps with a fine-point pen, a meticulous practice that almost ruined his ability to paint creatively. He returned to Reno once more in the 1950s, but in the next decade he moved to a farmhouse in the Connecticut Berkshires, where he worked on increasingly eccentric art projects until his death.

Much of Caples's artistic life was spent in thrall to the desert landscape. He wasn't interested in painting a topographically accurate depiction of it but, like Dixon, an increasing reduction of it to its essential elements, what he called "subjective naturalism," which in its manipulation of space is not so far from Dixon's "cubist realism." Although no one would ever mistake a Caples landscape for a Dixon, the graphic lessons both learned while painting murals is one obvious commonality. *Red Mountain,* a pastel on paper tentatively dated 1941, takes a vantage point at the edge of a playa, wind whipping across the flats and the mountains across the valley. Although the profile of the mountain doesn't match those of the Fox Range across the Smoke Creek from Moore's place, Caples could have made the picture while sitting with us on the Behemoth, so accurately has he captured the spirit of the conditions.

Marcia Growdon, who curated an exhibition of Caples's work at the Nevada Art Museum in 1982, pointed out that his early work demonstrated an assimilation of landscape abstraction by major American artists such as Stuart Davis and John Marin, but that he was also influenced by regionalists Thomas Hart Benton and Grant Wood. Exactly the same could have been said of Dixon. Traces of these stylistic influences are evident in Caples's paintings of Virginia City from the 1930s, where individual buildings and profiles of the mountains are recognizable but the entire view is compressed into an airless, mythical space that transcends even the planar flatness achieved by Dixon. Regarding the work Caples did later in his career, Growdon remarks that "In the 1950s and 1960s he created elegant, haunting distillations of the desert, mountains, and dramatic atmospheric effects experienced in the desert. Space is at once telescoped and expanded infinitely. The substance of the mountains and the volume of air are sucked out in favor of the essence of mountains and glowing atmospheric effects."

Another artist who would come west to Nevada and paint the playas during the mid-twentieth century was Craig Sheppard (1913–1978). Born in Oklahoma only six years after the territory had become a state, he was raised within physical and temporal reach of its frontier as a young cowboy and rodeo rider. When it came time to go to college, however, Sheppard swallowed hard and made the decision to be an art major at the University of Oklahoma in Norman. The department in those days was still run as a progressive series of classes in perspective and anatomy, a classical course of study that would virtually disappear from academia after World War II. Sheppard made friends with the young Indian artists in the program, who became known as the Kiowa Five, and, with the Depression then in full force, painted panoramic murals for extra cash.

After graduation, Sheppard received local mural commissions and was able to teach briefly at Oklahoma, then at Montana State University in Bozeman for two years before being pulled into the war effort as a technical draftsman for Douglas Aircraft in Tulsa. He returned to teaching as soon as he could, and 1947 found him at the University of Nevada in Reno, in charge of its new art department, where he would stay until his retirement. This, too, was a frontier in its own way, the beginning of the postwar boom in university art programs and increasing careerism for artists, as well as the establishment of the National Endowment for the Arts and the state arts agencies. Sheppard expanded his department faculty from two to seven by 1965 and

served as the first chairman of the Nevada Arts Council, his administrative and teaching duties often diverting him from painting, now a
familiar complaint in the art world.

Shortly after his arrival in Nevada, Sheppard stated to his close friend,
the novelist Robert Laxalt, that "colors in Nevada are invisible." His
colleague in the art department, printmaker Jim McCormick, quotes
Sheppard's wife, the sculptor Yolanda Jacobson, who noted that Sheppard "couldn't paint the desert properly for a couple of years." This
was a cognitive difficulty that McCormick, a fellow Oklahoman hired
by the older artist, also experienced when first moving to the state.
Sheppard was nonetheless seduced by the Nevada desert, bringing to
it a sense of earthy color and formal composition derived from his
classical training and the flat renderings of the world used by both the
Kiowa Five and the WPA muralists.

Sheppard made numerous excursions out onto the playas, and in
1971 the University of Nevada Press published a portfolio it had commissioned, *Landmarks of the Emigrant Trail.* The artist spent more
than a year making trips out into the desert with Yolanda, tracing six
hundred miles along the Applegate-Lassen Cutoff and across the
Black Rock, following the entries in Bruff's 1849 journal. He also traveled the playas with another author friend, Sessions S. Wheeler, and
together they produced what for years has remained one of the few
books about the area, *Nevada's Black Rock Desert,* which Sheppard
helped illustrate with paintings depicting the history of the region.
Working mostly in oils during his early career, toward the end of his
life he concentrated almost exclusively on watercolors, painting plein-
air in the sagebrush.

Sheppard was an accomplished artist who, like Caples, wasn't con-
tent to settle on one recognizable style. Both artists suffer from critical
neglect as a result. He experimented with abstraction throughout his
midcareer but is most remembered locally for his paintings depicting
the history of the region—prospectors, wagonmasters, sheepherders,
cowboys in their yellow rain slickers, everyone out working in the

desert. The paintings weren't usually narrative in the strictest sense but were painted in a style strongly influenced by the midwestern social realism of Benton and others, a style also favored by a contemporary of Sheppard's, Alexander Hogue, who taught McCormick at the University of Tulsa.

On the top fourth of the cover to Wheeler's Black Rock book, part of a Sheppard watercolor of the playa and its eponymous peak is reproduced in color, the painting in its entirety appearing in black and white on page 51. The pale flat playa is the level foreground of objective observation, the dust devils racing off to the left portrayed with a delicate, accurate transparency. The mountain itself, though accurate in outline, is abstracted from the context of the surrounding range, making it a stronger graphic element. Bearing down from the upper-right corner is a dark storm cloud, falling toward the playa as if it were about to bury it. Put next to Caples's *Red Mountain,* the paintings appear as if they were twin bookends to a lecture on the geomorphology of playas, as well as on the evolution of landscape representation in art.

A few things in common among these painters should by now be apparent. They all have a foot in pictorial representation, in the practice of reproducing accurately how we mentally construct the visual world, a way of looking at, remembering, and reconstructing it that is closely related to cartography. I don't mean that these artists applied a rigid grid to the world, though certainly Dixon and Sheppard, in particular, were schooled in various classical ways of dividing canvases mathematically in order to aid composition. Rather, they were adept at organizing the world visually so they could do more than just paint it—they could navigate through parts of it that most people find difficult to see clearly.

I would argue that a strong topographical ability helped these artists to cope both professionally and personally with the playas upon which they spent so much time. They may have abstracted the landscape, but their paintings have definite ties to specific places, ones they could name with precision. Speaking with Michael Moore about his life, he is likewise precise and thorough about where he's traveled in Nevada, what the landscape looks like in every location, even twenty years afterward. Dixon and Sheppard and Caples seem to have shared some of that ability to varying degrees, comfortable with traveling alone into unknown territory, knowing they could bring back mental maps and images allowing them to travel freely back and forth from studio to playa, in fact and in imagination.

All three artists found themselves abstracting the landscape to one degree or another. They moved beyond representation, which in and of itself is not a simple matter, and into the extraction of specific landscape elements in order to compose paintings that addressed an underlying, ineffable spirituality that they felt in the desert. It's a process observed clearly in the work of many landscape painters, but nowhere more so than in the paintings of J. M. W. Turner, who is worth a short digression, given his direct and indirect influences on these artists.

Born in 1775 and trained at an early age as a topographical draftsman in the studio of an architectural viewmaker, Turner's main hobby was hiking, and he wandered the countryside making sketches that he later turned into watercolors. By the time he was twenty-one, he was entering exquisitely detailed architectural paintings in the annual Royal Academy exhibition. In 1800, after seeing two paintings the previous year by the landscape classicist Claude Lorrain, he turned to painting historical pictures. Within three years, critics were complaining that he had drifted too far from the imitation of reality, that his paintings were becoming too wild. They hadn't seen anything yet.

Slashing at his canvas with a loaded palette knife, in 1810 Turner painted *Cottage Destroyed by an Avalanche,* wherein a tumultuous mass of white paint tumbles from the upper right-hand of the picture and overwhelms the landscape, a great rock thrust by the snow upon a wooden cottage as if it were the head of a hammer (the same compositional strategy used by Sheppard in the Black Rock painting). The surface of the paint—square patches of white laid directly off the palette knife like blocks of ice—is implicated in the avalanche, Turner pushing his technique beyond what was then accepted pictorial practice. It's a great example of the romantic sublime, but still only a harbinger of what would come in 1812 when Turner painted *Snow Storm: Hannibal Crossing the Alps*. Ostensibly a history painting by its title, on the canvas swirling dark storm clouds literally destroy the landscape behind the figures cowering in the foreground. The painting is composed according to Golden Sections, the most common classical division of visual space, but the geometry is subsumed by a vortex of paint, which viewers can't fail to equate with the violence of the natural world.

As John Walker points out on his book about Turner, in the 1830s and 1840s Turner created paintings the likes of which would not be seen again for a century, when the abstract expressionists came to the foreground of American painting. The landscapes are so abstract, so bathed in light and shadow, that they approach what some later critics propose to be a genuine balance between objective observation of the external world with subjective inner vision. Writers at the time, save John Ruskin, thought that Turner's style had merely degenerated into insanity.

In a later painting also titled *Snow Storm,* one from 1842, Turner came to the edge of what can be expressed. He gave a lengthy caption to the painting when it was first exhibited, *Steamboat off a Harbour's Mouth making signals in shallow water, and going by the lead. The author was in this storm on the night the Ariel left Harwitch,* which was an attempt to provide his audience with some kind of objective correlative. Lashed to the mast of the ship for four hours during the storm in order to observe its force, he returned with a picture not just of a meteorological event but of cognition itself. In a sense, the critics were right. Turner was stretching visual sanity as it was then known, exploring the boundary where the vocabulary of painting became inarticulate utterance. It wasn't just that his scenes of violent nature were awe-inspiring and filled with terror; so was his balancing act on the tightrope of art.

Turner died in December 1851, having achieved the status of what art historian Andrew Wilton labeled the "Topographer of Sublimities," and it's hard to imagine that any landscape painter since has been unaffected by his work. Thomas Moran (1837–1926), to give a relevant example, first traveled to England in 1862 specifically to study and copy Turner's landscapes. He would return six more times, often retracing Turner's hikes in order to correlate specific locations to the paintings and to decide for himself how to tackle his own sublime landscapes. Returning to America, he would then apply the techniques Turner used in painting the Alps and the Scottish Highlands to Yellowstone and the Grand Canyon.

Moran, in turn, has always been of decisive interest to those artists in the West seeking to represent its landscape, whether in a pictorial mode or in a more heightened manner, seeking to understand not just what we see in the world, but how. Which at last brings us back to the playas and the paintings of Michael Moore, although Moore personally is more a fan of Moran's work than of Turner's.

Moore was born in 1942 and lived with his grandparents in San Mateo during World War II, while his father was a radarman in the U.S. Navy. From when he was eight until fourteen, he lived in La Cañada in the foothills outside Los Angeles, making his first trip to Death Valley with a photographer who lived in town, a climber and proto-environmentalist who introduced Moore to both the desert and the high mountains of the eastern Sierra. Not a particularly disciplined student, Moore was sent to the private Webb School in Claremont, another town at the foot of the San Gabriel Mountains, graduating in 1960 with a Bank of America award in art and acceptance into Stanford University.

Moore had been sketching vernacular architecture—sheds and shacks, for the most part—since La Cañada, and with his dad, an early member of the legendary San Onofre Surf Club, he had become in the 1950s a devotee of the ten-foot-long surfboards of the time. Stanford's art department was unable to exercise much of a hold on him the first time he tried it, and he took two quarters off to work in manufacturing and to surf. When it became apparent that the world of commerce was seriously overrated as a lifestyle, he returned to Stanford, where in his absence the entire art faculty had turned over. He wrangled himself a position as slide projectionist for the new art history professor, Albert Elsen, and found himself exposed to influences beyond Franz Kline, Willem De Kooning, and Jackson Pollock, the reigning abstract expressionists he had earlier admired. Now he added California's own hard-edge painters, such as Keith Boyle and the geometrically inclined Ron Davis, as well as that supreme landscape abstractionist, Richard Diebenkorn.

In 1964 he was accepted into the Yale MFA program, the pinnacle of achievement for an aspiring painter of the time. Perhaps the artist most influential on Moore's work while in New Haven, however, wasn't anyone on the faculty, but Llyn Foulkes, a Los Angeles Pop artist who was living in Topanga Canyon and known for making paintings of anonymous places. Moore found himself constructing a series of album pictures based on the road trip he'd taken to get from California to Connecticut, his first big driving trip, and one undertaken in a 1959 Plymouth station wagon that he remembers with fondness. In somewhat the same vein as Dixon and Caples, the young artist still found schooling, if not irrelevant, at least too constraining. He stayed in the Yale program for only a year, then hung around New Haven for another, at one point getting his lifestyle down to such minimal possessions that his landlord thought he'd moved out and was showing his place to prospective renters when he came home one afternoon.

Moore, missing the West, headed back to California in May 1966 and bounced back and forth between L.A. and Palo Alto before settling into the Haight-Ashbury District of San Francisco, where he eventually made a living painting houses, signs, and murals, and crafting furniture out of old auto parts. Although he was continuing to paint, two events seem to have rescued him from what could have become a lifelong downward spiral into perpetual hippiedom. In spring of 1967, while still living in Palo Alto, he took a long driving trip with friends up through Cedarville in Northern California, then east through the northwest quadrant of Nevada to Denio, a small town on the arid Nevada-Oregon border. Thirty-five years later, there still aren't many paved roads in that part of Nevada, which is so remote that it's home to the Sheldon National Wildlife Range, a sanctuary for the once nearly extinct pronghorn, a western American version of the antelope. They wandered up to Idaho's Craters of the Moon, the severity of their scenery explicit in the name, and witnessed a thunderstorm over Pyramid Lake, very definitely an experience in the category of the romantic sublime. Ten years later, he was still trying to retrace parts of the trip, so vivid were his memories of it.

The other event was a trip he took back to New Haven in 1968, where some former classmates had formed PULSA, an environmental art research group fooling around with early computers, sleep deprivation, and attempts to emulate through light and sound the changes in consciousness that drugs produced. This artistic alchemy was being attempted on campuses across the country, and it provided Mike a chance to meet David Rumsey, who would become a lifelong friend, collaborator, and collector of his work, as well as a real-estate impresario able to make the Smoke Creek property a reality some years later.

Moore returned west in the summer of 1969, passing through the LIBRE commune in southern Colorado and meeting Linda Fleming, one of its cofounders. She doesn't remember seeing him there, and it would take seventeen years for them to bump into each other again. All this driving around, however, was creating the inevitable addiction, and he found himself out in the desert almost every spring and fall thereafter. By 1971, he was leaving found objects out on the remote northeast corner of Pyramid Lake, doing silkscreens of desert scenes based on photos, and making progressively larger landscape paintings.

The PULSA group came out to do residencies at Cal Arts and Mills College throughout the early 1970s, taking a break from the late-winter snows of Connecticut, and Moore took David Rumsey out into the desert. It must have been a life-changing experience for the latter, because he relocated a few years later to the Bay Area and became an habitué of Nevada. In 1974, Moore had a substantial show at the Stanford University Art Gallery, and through 1978 he had what he calls "a nice little career blip" selling his work, which by now had gotten as large as five-by-twenty-foot color-washed landscape triptychs.

In 1978, his first marriage fell apart and he moved into the basement of a building owned by Rumsey, supporting himself by working on one of his friend's renovation projects across the street. Familiar by this time with Maynard Dixon's work and identifying strongly with the idea of having studios in both the city and the desert, it wasn't yet an idea he could realize. Moore took time off to trek the Khumbu region of Nepal near Mount Everest in 1979, started doing abstract paintings, and in 1981 even tried a stint back east, living in Connecticut and commuting into New York City to support himself with renovation work. The next year he started going back out into the desert with Rumsey, this time looking for some property to buy. They weren't sure how serious they were about the idea, but it was a good excuse for road trips, and they quartered Northern Nevada in search of suitable sites. In fall of 1984, Moore and Rumsey bought a forty-acre mountaintop outside Winnemucca, the site of an abandoned radar installation 2,300 feet above the valley floor. The eight-hundred-square-foot windowless building that housed the air force equipment was still there, along with a 10' x 14' miner's shack that became his studio. What else could he call it but "Radar Ranch," a pun off the old Gene Autry sci-fi western? He was living in the sort of vernacular West he had first traveled through and drawn as a kid.

Moore now radically changed his relationship to the desert; instead of seeing how many miles he could drive every day on dirt roads, he went to testing how few he could manage, holed up on the mountain and making one small painting after another of the views. In 1986 he again ran into Linda Fleming, who was now teaching at the San Francisco Art Institute. Like Michael, she was not only a desert aficionado, but having lived on the LIBRE commune for years, where she'd built her own house from scratch, she was well equipped to take on improvements to Radar Ranch. In 1990 they built a studio on the ridge there, so that Linda would have a summer work space as well, and for several years they braved the dirt road up the mountain every spring in a tough four-wheel-drive Chevy truck.

Unlike Dixon, Caples, and Sheppard, all of whom worked not only in landscape but also in figurative work and even portraiture at times, Moore has mostly limited his work to the land as a subject, and although there are numerous strands one can follow in the development of his *oeuvre,* perhaps the most consistent one is relationship to the horizon, that long line we tend to read from left to right as if it were a sentence. We can begin with a work painted in 1967, *The Perfect Image of a Priest,* an acrylic-on-canvas painted as if from the viewpoint of a surfer in the water looking at the coastline of California.

When gazing at the very nearly white surface of the square painting, which has three rough tawny bands of ocher, tan, russet, sienna, and umber running across it, the piece resembles nothing so much as a coastal profile made by that eighteenth-century English painter, William Hodges, who sailed with Cook during his second voyage across the Pacific Ocean in 1772 to 1775. Examining *The Perfect Image of a Priest,* you can imagine yourself sitting on a surfboard and attempting to maintain position by triangulating yourself from features on the shore. That's an essential skill for a surfer who is attempting to hold a fixed position between sets of swells above whatever invisible topography of the seafloor will produce the best waves relative to the size and direction of the swells and the wind that day. It's sophisticated intuitive navigation, and a talent applicable to maintaining a sense of self when out on a playa. Coastal profiles are likewise relevant.

This painting by Moore isn't a literal coastal profile, however, but an impression by him of how landscape is perceived. He was stacking three separate examples on top of each other, and thinking as much about the desert outside Barstow, California, as he was the coast when he composed it. As such, it's an early example of Moore attempting to understand how we see and mentally construct large spaces.

In *From the Windy Place* (1986), a landscape verging on the abstract that Moore painted in homage to the view from a perennial campsite above the Smoke Creek, the playa far beneath him has been reduced to an empty band of light ground framed between brown mountains defining a horizon and almost black hills in the foreground. Sky fills nearly the top two-thirds of the canvas. The painting is almost schematic in its analysis of the landforms, generalized away from the specificity of a profile and toward a mural-like abstraction. By 1989, Moore was painting his remarkable *Phenomenon* works, which show tall dust devils waltzing across the desert floor and columns of smoke rising from range fires. The views are elevated and the flat floor of Nevada has become a stage set for dramatic incidence.

If you page through the hundreds of small watercolor works Moore has cranked out since having a studio in the desert, sometimes completing as many as fifty or sixty in a two-week period, whether he's in Nevada, summering at Linda's old place in Colorado, or even working from memory when elsewhere, you can see him practicing not so much the hand-eye coordination that drawings might facilitate but a fine-tuning of the mind-hand relationship. Because of the cognitive dissonance we experience in the immense expanses of the playas, this is a more critical skill than simple representation, more than just transferring landscape to paper. What has to be examined, if one is to survive successfully in the desert, much less paint it, is not just how we see but how we think up the landscape.

By the mid-1990s, these strands came together quite forcefully in Moore's work. One of his better-known paintings is *Black Rock Desert, October 6, 1996*, which was used by the University of Georgia

Press for the cover of a book of poems by David Rumsey's daughter, Tessa. Instead of the sky dominating the top half or two-thirds of the picture plane, it's been reduced to only the top quarter, a band of cool and nearly indeterminate color that recedes behind a horizon of subtly variegated hills contained horizontally very much, again, like a topographical profile. The remainder of the canvas, its bottom three-quarters, is dominated by the surface of the dry lake, which has been built up in typical Moore fashion from wet layers of acrylic. The painting is at once a bold graphic statement and an accurate depiction of how the flat ground continually draws down our gaze.

What focuses the picture is an interruption in that single dark band of the horizon, an oblong of white fuzziness within which hovers a dark dot, a tiny shape echoed on the ground beneath it. It appears to be headed toward the viewer, a vehicle driving across the playa, suspended in midair and disconnected from the earth by mirage. Pictured in any other landscape, the situation would appear surreal. As a depiction of how vision works in the desert, however, the composition is nearly literal. That tension between how we think things work in landscape paintings and what Moore is doing in his work is an analog for how our perceptual apparatus interacts with the desert, and it lifts the value of his work immeasurably.

The late 1990s saw Moore continually integrating and recombining the starkly disparate visual forms of the Smoke Creek playa and other desert vistas in large landscape paintings, sometimes juxtaposing two or even three separate views onto one canvas. He's fully aware of Dixon's work, and also Michael Heizer's. Heizer, in fact, made his sculpture *Dissipate 1*, five "earth removals," out on the Smoke Creek in 1968, then immediately thereafter *Dissipate 2* on the Black Rock, both parts of the *Nine Nevada Depressions*. Moore's horizontally banded view titled *Two Nevada Depressions*, which stacks one playa and profiled horizon above the other, is a direct allusion, the playas themselves now serving as the actual depressions.

Moore has never been much of either an ab-ex-er or a hard-edge painter—his subject matter is too literal for the former and his handling of paint too fluid for the latter. He's not a conceptualist, a minimalist, a neo-geo, or a member of any number of other late-twentieth-century art cliques. Instead, he is a painter who has developed a specific visual vocabulary for representing how his mind organizes the Big Empty. There are artistic precedents to Michael's work in nineteenth-century topographical pictures, in the paintings of Dixon and Caples and Sheppard, and he has followed their tendency to abstract desert landforms, to shuffle them into a formal order that nonetheless admits onto the picture plain the randomizing elements of weather and human presence.

But while standing and looking out through the double glass doors that lead out of what may become either a living room or a painting studio—Linda and Michael have yet to decide—he tells me: "For years I've been working on nonlinear perspective. I've been looking at pattern density instead, for instance, and atmospheric perspective because there's so much ambiguity of scale here."

"Today's a good example," he says, pointing out across the playa. The cloud shadows moving across its surface are so dark they're almost three-dimensional. "You look out there and a certain amount of contrast exists. Then, when you look back, there's less. Or sometimes more. It reverses because of where the light is, and different areas advance or disappear, depending. The playa, which should be most in focus because it's the closest, gets washed out, while the mountains are in sharp relief."

Not only do I see what he's talking about while we're looking outside, but thinking about the paintings, now I see that he's pinning down examples of these conditions one by one where we can actually understand what we're seeing, versus standing confusedly in the middle of it.

Burning Man   Black Rock Desert

I'm sitting here on the great playa of the Black Rock Desert with my twenty-six-year-old son, Tarn, and surrounded by roughly 25,451 of our closest friends, all of us gathered together for the annual celebration of the Burning Man. Our camp consists of an olive-green surplus parachute underneath which reside numerous nylon chairs, folding tables, two double-burner gas stoves, coolers of fresh meat and vegetables, and boxes stuffed with an assortment of fine wines and spirits. Tarn is humming to himself, this assemblage exactly the sort of Hemingway-on-safari scene he had envisioned, and one diametrically opposed to our usual setup, which consists of a single tent, two sleeping bags, and a tiny mountaineering stove.

While he's been enjoying the newfound luxuries of such elaborate car-camping, I've been thinking about both where we are—the four hundred square miles that are one of the largest unimpeded flat places on our continent—and its antithesis, the great anti-playa of the Salton Sea in Southern California, which I had visited this summer with his younger brother, Mat. I'm also keeping a wary eye on the parachute, which we've stretched between our rented white Chevy van and Jonah Loop's black suv. The wind is gusting up to thirty miles per hour, and the nylon chute, which was already ripped when we purchased it for $69 at an army-surplus store in Reno, flaps incessantly overhead, slowly fraying itself into oblivion.

Jonah is one of Tarn's oldest friends, and despite our roof blustering as if it might blow out, he sits back calmly in one of the blue camp chairs, smoking a cigarette while Walter Grey fusses with brunch ingredients over our twin Coleman stoves. Jonah is the founder of a small digital special-effects firm in Northern California that caters to Hollywood producers making large-budget action films, which fits neatly into his obsession with the newest and fastest computers, massively quick motorcycles, precision-engineered knives that open with little more than a flick of a thumb, and fencing. It's a lifestyle based on

power and speed harnessed to aesthetics, and one that could come directly out of a contemporary Japanese *anime* feature.

Walter, who tops out around six-foot-seven and has twin thunder-bolts tattooed down his back, fishes a deadly looking blade out of his jeans pocket to attack a package of sausage. A former member of the armed forces, as well as a short-order cook, Walter is affable if some-what impenetrable, and known to carry a staggeringly large sidearm about his person, which he has put aside in the spirit of the occasion. He's also a graduate of the California College of Arts and Crafts and enrolled as an architecture student at the University of Washington. In sum, exactly the sort of twenty-nine-year-old you'd expect to find at the world's largest playa event, a festival of art and what the Burners call "radical self-expression."

Laurel Roth completes our party. At a willowy six feet, and with cheekbones high enough for her to be a runway model in New York, she is nonetheless just short of shy, carefully pragmatic, and deliberate in her motions. She has, quite sensibly, had her brunette hair tightly braided beforehand into more than thirty strands, thus obviating the need to wash it during the multiple wind-and-dust storms that have been blowing through camp. A five-time attendee of Burning Man, she is a former crew supervisor for the Marin Conservation Corps and knows her way around a campsite. Like Jonah and Walter, she carries a knife lethal-looking enough to scare off casual gadflies, and she proudly drives a motorcycle fast enough to propel the living shit out of most people.

Tarn and I have had tickets to Burning Man since the spring in order for me to include the event in this book on playas. The others weren't planning on coming, but Walter and Jonah inherited a couple of tickets less than two weeks ago from Michael Hefflin, another friend in the circle, who was killed while riding a motorcycle that once belonged to Walter. The knife that Walter is using to open the sausage, in fact, was Michael's. Whenever he pulls it out, which is often, razor-honed German steel being second nature to this group, everyone tends to fall silent.

I slip outside the canopy to check on the weather and to gather my thoughts in the van about how the Slab City community near the Salton Sea relates to the Black Rock and Burning Man. The week has turned unseasonably cold, thin bands of storm clouds marching in prematurely from the Gulf of Alaska—a pattern that normally doesn't set up in Nevada until late October or early November. It even sprinkled early this morning, the precipitation not enough to create mud, but it did temporarily close up the small cracks in the playa surface that otherwise make it seem as if we're camped on top of an immense jigsaw puzzle. To my right, I can see old shorelines of the ancient Lake Lahontan marching up the Granite Range. The waters here were once five hundred feet deep, the last of the intact lake evaporating only six thousand years ago. Since then, the climate has remained for the most part much warmer and drier, contrary to the evidence this morning.

Winds accompanying this type of weather pattern often stir up great clouds of dust from the Smoke Creek playa, which first become visible from here as a brown haze spreading over Gerlach, the nearest town, which is twelve miles to the southwest. Fifteen or twenty minutes later, as the dust storms reach the western edge of Burning Man City, which is precisely where we're camped, the day turns dark. When the initial wave of dust hits the parachute, everyone freezes for a few seconds to assess the severity. If it's thick enough, which usually doesn't happen until midafternoon, people pull kerchiefs up over their noses in order to breathe. Despite the alkali whiteouts that reduce visibility down to a couple of feet, however, it's actually a relief from the smoke of the forest fires through which I've been driving and hiking all summer, tens of thousands of wildfires consuming more than 1.5 million acres of the western United States. Burning Man is the fitting cap to such an apocalyptic season.

While I'm assessing the clouds, a tanker truck rolls slowly by, spraying water on the city's semicircular "streets" to settle the dust. In the other direction, one of the two sanitation pumpers leaves after having cleaned out some of the 350 portable toilets scattered throughout the gathering. I watch a highway patrol car cruise by, as well as vehicles from the Bureau of Land Management and the local sheriff's office, and two of our own Black Rock Rangers on bicycles. The deep level of organization all this implies is what makes it possible for personal anarchies to fluoresce out here for even so brief a period as a week.

Started as an intimate torching of an eight-foot-high figure in San Francisco in September 1986 by Larry Harvey, a local artist, the event was moved to the Black Rock in 1990 in order to accommodate the growing crowds that insisted on attending what was fast becoming a seasonal ritual. Like the burning of Old Man Zozobra in Santa Fe and various neo-Celtic rituals consummated in the autumn, people took Burning Man as a vehicle in which they could declare summer to be over and the winter of work about to begin. Silicon Valley, the most task-obsessed locale in North America, now virtually shuts down for the event, at least half of the attendees here having a spectacular blowout on vintage wines, vodka, and single-malt scotches, on psychedelic mushrooms and acid and marijuana brownies, on nudity and rave dancing and massive pyrotechnics—before returning to their cramped gray cubicles in which they attempt to invent the dot.com future.

I'd come to Burning Man only once before, in 1992, when six hundred of us camped out on the playa in a circle around a forty-foot-tall wooden armature that for the first time that year was outlined in blue neon tubing, which small noisy generators powered each night. Art projects were scattered around campsites, and Richard Misrach stalked good shots in the late-afternoon light. When a small plane flipped upon its landing nearby and the occupants staggered unhurt from the upside-down cabin, they were greeted with hugs and goblets of wine. At midnight, as the Man was torched after several hours of eating and drinking, intense drumming, singing, and dancing, we all proceeded to circle the embers clockwise in a kind of trance. Who needed drugs? The sight of a bare-chested man wearing a stag's head and baying at the fire was neolithic enough to send you shivering into another universe.

Things got a little out of hand the next few years, the crowds growing from 2,000 in 1994 to 10,000 in 1997, and finally this year to cross the threshold of what the U.S. Census Bureau defines as a city, 25,000 people. For the week it's occupied, Burning Man becomes the fifth largest city in the state. In the past, the event has hosted a drive-by shooting range for automatic weapons (a practice now outlawed by the organizers), free-ranging road races across the playa (likewise forbidden since a fatal accident), and fireworks powerful enough to send small rockets halfway to the moon (also curtailed). In short, as things here have gotten larger, the Burning Man organization has separated out some of the crazier and more lethal aspects from the crowd. Still, my ticket reads as follows:

> YOU VOLUNTARILY ASSUME THE RISK
> OF SERIOUS INJURY OR DEATH BY ATTENDING
> You must bring enough food, water, shelter, and first aid to survive one week in a harsh desert environment. Commercial vending, fire-arms, fireworks, rockets and all other explosives prohibited. You agree to read and abide by all rules in the Survival Guide. You agree to follow federal, state and local laws. This is a LEAVE NO TRACE, Pack it in, Pack it OUT event. You are asked to contribute 2 hours of playa clean up before departure. Commercial use of im-ages taken at Burning Man is prohibited without the prior written consent of Burning Man. You appoint Burning Man as your repre-sentative to take actions necessary to protect your intellectual property or privacy rights, recognizing that Burning Man has no obligation to take any action whatsoever.
> PARTICIPATE

I actually find this language reassuring, recognizing its roots in such science-fiction novels as *The Moon Is a Harsh Mistress* by that master of the genre, Robert A. Heinlein, who, as he got older, turned increas-ingly to the conundrum of how to devise a government under which a social contract could be honored yet "radical self-expression" would be preserved. The Mars novels of Kim Stanley Robinson deal with the same issues, desert planets being ideal stages for the play of great ideas.

The utopian experiments and literature that undergird the spirit of Burning Man also found expression in the Salton Sink during the twentieth century, although there the organizers drove down a fork in the road leading to real-estate development. Burning Man is orga-nized successfully as a nonprofit entity, its $3.4-million annual budget devoted mostly to providing infrastructure, from a trash fence that runs around the entire five square miles of the camp to water trucks to keep down the dust on the streets that the volunteer Department of Public Works lays out each year. By contrast, the scheme for the playa that would become the Salton Sea, the largest lake in California, was centered around a fable of profit that collapsed on almost everyone involved, except for corporate agribusiness. And the denizens of Slab City.

No two playas I've visited are exactly the same, but the Salton Sea is stretching the point about as far as it can be taken. First of all, the underlying geology is different, the sink sitting at the lowest point in the Salton Trough, an elongated depression 170 miles long by 70 miles wide. At its lower end, the trough runs underneath the Gulf of California, which at one time extended northward to the base of the San Bernardino Mountains, about where Palm Springs is located today. The Colorado River, then entering the ocean near what would later be Fort Yuma, built up a silty delta that eventually closed off the upper end of the gulf and created the prehistoric Lake Cahuilla, a body of water that over millennia was refreshed as the river flooded the Salton Sink but that evaporated down to a playa in dry years. Geologists refer to the area as a "terminal sink basin," and the last time the lake finally receded was probably between A.D. 1400 and 1500.

The Colorado was known during the nineteenth century to intermittently flood the playa that was left behind, the bottom of which sits 275 feet or so below sea level, but that didn't stop early land speculators from carving a canal from the river into the Salton Sink in order to promote agriculture. Unfortunately, and as William deBuys points out in his superb book on the region, *Salt Dreams,* in their rush to riches the speculators constructed a supplementary ditch fifty feet wide and seven feet deep in 1904 to sip more quickly from the river — a trench with no head gate or flood controls whatsoever, though they knew the Colorado could increase its flow by as much as a hundredfold. Their timing couldn't have been more spectacular: 1905–1906 turned into some of the wettest El Niño years ever recorded.

The first flood came in February 1905, followed by a second, but it wasn't until the third flood in March of that year that the directors of the California Development Company realized they were having a problem and tried to erect a brush dam around pilings to plug the ditch. This was perhaps not the ideal choice of material. The Colorado ate the dam, the pilings, and the surrounding banks, greatly increasing its flow into the sink as it cut a minor version of the Grand Canyon in the process. It flooded the local saltworks and even forced relocation of the Southern Pacific's railroad tracks to higher ground. It wasn't until February 1907, after the river had subsided and 80,000 cubic yards of rock had been dumped into the ditch, that the flood was halted. By then the sink was covered with a lake forty miles long by thirteen wide, which inundated five hundred square miles and was eighty-five feet deep—the largest lake in the state. As far as I know, this is the most dramatic reconversion of a playa into a lake anywhere in the world.

Today, this anti-playa, the Salton Sea, covers about 381 square miles, having achieved an uneasy balance between evaporation and replenishment from agricultural runoff and sewage, streams of which run into it from the farms and fields at its northwest and southeastern ends. The Coachella and Imperial valleys are the most intensively irrigated lands in America, and among the most productive agricultural lands on the planet, but the excess water leaching downhill into the Salton Sea is loaded with a potent brew of chemical fertilizers and insecticides, as well as naturally occurring selenium, which is three times more poisonous to humans than arsenic.

As a result, the waters of the thirty-six-mile-long lake are 25 percent saltier than those of the Pacific Ocean, fish by the millions are suffocated in algae blooms, and the shoreline is littered with the remnants of failed yacht clubs and subdivisions. Corporate agribusiness has flourished, but it caused the local real-estate business to fold and the new ecosystem to collapse. During the summer of 1996, an outbreak of avian botulism on the lake killed roughly a third of the entire population of the endangered brown pelicans, the carcasses of more than 1,100 brown and 8,500 white pelicans shoveled into incinerators before they could create yet another layer of health hazard.

Photographers such as Misrach, Joan Myers, and Christopher Landis have for years documented what is one of the world's more surreal environmental and economic devastations, and one not likely to be remedied soon. Freshening the waters with inflow from the Colorado, for instance, was estimated in the summer of 2000 to cost upward of a billion dollars. Draining the lake, or simply letting it evaporate, would create an airborne selenium hazard that would play severe havoc with the health of people living downwind for hundreds of miles.

Like most of the playas of the American West, water-covered or not, the Salton Sink has been used by the military. The Navy's Salton Sea Test Base covers only 1,945 acres of land, but includes 13,642 acres of water on its southwest corner, and during World War II it was used as a base for seaplanes and as a bombing range. From 1945 through 1961, the base was run by the Atomic Energy Commission for classified research; this no doubt gives people serving in the Army Corps of Engineers, which is responsible for cleaning up the now-decommissioned base, some pause.

To the east, just on the other side of the hamlet of Niland (population 1,042) was situated the 640-acre Camp Dunlap, a World War II U.S. Marine Corps training facility. All that's left are forty rectangular concrete foundations, referred to now collectively as "Slab City," but despite the lack of water, sewage, or power hookups, that's just enough core infrastructure to attract a handful of full-time residents and a seasonal population of between five to ten thousand temporary squatters, 90 percent of whom are over the age of sixty, and all of whom are escaping rent. If the planned real-estate developments failed to work out as hoped, this ad hoc one based on self-governance and a barter economy has flourished.

In July, my younger son, Mat, and I toured the slabs, perching on the concrete to have lunch during one of those more than 110 days of the year when the temperature exceeds a hundred degrees. Slab City, at 141 feet below sea level and shaded only by the mesquite and tamarisks that manage to survive on an average of two and a half inches of rainfall a year, is not much of a garden spot. We saw no more than a couple of dozen parked vehicles, plus the paranoid-chic quarters of some pre-apocalyptic warriors barricaded behind bristling fences and shrouded in camouflage netting.

From November through March, though, when an estimated one million senior snowbirds are circulating on the interstates and other asphalt byways of America, cruising just ahead of the frost line and looking for places to congregate, Slab City becomes a maze of RVs, trailers, vans, tents—actually, as I look around our Black Rock encampment this morning, very much like the vehicular smorgasbord that comprises the Burning Man Festival.

Among the hundred or so permanent residents of Slab City are those who make, if not a living, then at least a recreation out of retrieving scraps of freshly dropped munitions from the Chocolate Mountain Aerial Gunnery Range that stretches behind the old base. In theory and by law, the 400,000 acres of the bombing range that were set aside for the military the same year as those for the seaplane base across the valley are off limits to civilians. Past the slabs and up toward the Coachella Canal, which forms the boundary of the gunnery range, however, are dozens of well-used dirt roads heading east toward the mountains. DeBuys calls the persistent "scrappers" an odd "kind of cargo cult who pray for aluminum bomb and missile fins, high-alloy casings, machine gun clips, and other scrap from the sky."

It's as if Mad Max, that archetypal postapocalyptic desert mercenary, had come to life before Armageddon and settled in Southern California, a nice bookend to the pastel golfers taking their leisure in Palm Springs at the northern end of the valley. But Slab City and Burning Man share more than a vehicular aesthetic, a point driven home as Mat and I exited past Leonard Knight's Salvation Mountain, or what deBuys reports that the artist referred to as his "Bible Mountain Sculpt." A small mesa upon the face of which the sixty-nine-year-old man has poured more than sixty thousand gallons of paint since 1985, the primary message of this outsider earthwork proclaims that "God Is Love" (as well as displaying the inevitable American flag). Knight told deBuys that his artwork "stands out so much from the desert that pilots navigate by it," a nice twist on other directional aids offered the military across that cognitive wasteland of the desert.

What I'm thinking, of course, is how much all the playas—no matter how different their underlying geology and current conditions—have in common, and how places that offer severe cognitive dislocations both repel and attract us, perhaps a result of our neurobiology sensing that they are both dangerous and potentially interesting, hallmarks of territory for the taking. The word *mirage* not only conjures up the dangerous illusion that water may be pooled on the surface of the Black Rock but that money has likewise floated just outside the speculative marinas of the Salton Sea built in the 1950s.

Pre-apocalyptic gatherings on desert flats have long been a favorite preoccupation of the human race; the nomadic and biblical precedents are numerous, and in our own times they have manifested themselves into ad hoc tribal assemblies. When the space shuttle is scheduled to land at Edwards Air Force Base, for example, tens of thousands of people throng out to the playa and line up their RVS, vans, SUVS, and other assorted portable living spaces into gigantic celebratory camps, a phenomenon photographed by the seemingly omnipresent Misrach. Dozens of bands play country-and-western or rock music, souvenir stands spring up, and tailgate parties form an impromptu social circuit. It's a scene that's even been satirized in science-fiction movies, where innocent worshipers of aliens gather to witness a close encounter, only to be slaughtered with lethal green rays or captured with mind control, thus providing the scriptwriter, director, and studio pyrotechnicans an excuse to exercise their ingenuity in saving the human race from extinction or subjugation.

Coming through the Black Rock three years ago to work on an earlier book about the cognitive dissonance we cope with in large spaces, my friend Alvin McLane and I visited another mass gathering flooded with lookey-loos ourselves among them, the camp of a British team attempting to break both the land-speed record and the sound barrier. Andy Green, a former RAF fighter pilot, was exactly the right choice to drive the vehicle, a fifty-four-foot-long projectile powered by a matched pair of 110,000-horsepower jet engines.

The racing teams used to frequent the Bonneville Salt Flats International Speedway, which is where multiple land-speed records were set by Craig Breedlove of up to 600 miles per hour until 1965, but mineral extraction had not only dangerously thinned the salt crust, the speedway itself had begun to shrink in length. Fifteen miles long in 1950, it had gotten as short as ten miles before Reilly Industries started pumping brine back out onto the salt flats in 1997. The vehicles were simply getting too heavy and powerful for the Utah site, and when Richard Noble wanted to break Breedlove's record, he came to the Black Rock, where the surface was flatter and harder.

The English team fielded by Noble definitively shifted the racing scene to the Black Rock in 1985 by breaking Breedlove's record at just over 633 mph. At the time of our visit in 1997, Breedlove and Noble both had camps out on the southern end of the Black Rock and were going at it head to head. The combined size of the encampments, the number of onlookers, and the volume of media coverage for the playa event was exceeded only by that of Burning Man. Breedlove never got his car, the *Spirit of America,* anywhere near the speed of sound, which given the weather and altitude at the time was calculated to be 748.11 mph. Green piloted the Thrust ssc through the record and the sound barrier on October 15, blowing away both at 763.035 mph. One minute, the playa was empty; during the next, there was a muffled sonic boom and an alkali cloud eleven miles long.

Green's record still stands and may not be exceeded on the Black Rock for a while, given two factors. First, alkali dust is more easily handled by conventional engines than by jets, which are thrust-driven and thus suck in the ultra-fine particulates. Second, the Nevada playa is fragile in its own way, and the BLM isn't anxious to see it chewed up by too many speed trials.

The Black Rock, which each year now hosts a number of casual day users equal in number to festival attendees, is getting to be awfully busy for what is allegedly one of America's more remote locations, and the physical strain on its surface may be showing, at least in some years. During a wet winter or spring, the Quinn River overflows its banks from the northeast and sends a very shallow lake swelling across the playa. Pushed around by wind, the body of water, which can grow to be as large as fifty miles long by twenty wide, yet only five inches deep, polishes much of the surface back to its palimpsest-like nature. In a dry year, a broken crust may not be smoothed over, and some people speculate that Burning Man or the land-speed racers have created windblown dust that piles up and then hardens into small mounds up to a foot high, a recent feature on the playa.

John Bogard and friends of Planet X landsail out here on their three-wheeled dirtboats, and the "playa serpents," "desert snakes," or "reefs," as the low dunes have been variously labeled, are hazardous to their health, invisible as they are to anyone running at high speeds across the playa. Bogard has filed a complaint with the BLM about their not doing a full-blown Environmental Impact Statement of Burning Man, believing that the event has simply gotten too large for it to be held on a fickle surface that is, in essence, his backyard. The complaint alleges that fugitive dust from Burning Man piles up as the transient dunes, but the link of cause to effect is only conjecture at this point. It's as or more likely that the vastly increased OHV activity may have caused the dunes, or the Breedlove versus Noble/Green competition, or that they are even the result of some undetermined natural subsurface activity. Yet another theory in the Winnemucca Field Office of the Bureau of Land Management is that they were deposited by wind-driven water from flash floods. Whatever the cause, pictures of similar features that existed temporarily in the same area were taken as early as 1970.

It may be unfair of me to say so, but the creation of what a mountain climber would call an objective hazard on the surface of your recreation—such as the buildup of cornices prone to avalanching your route of ascent—is part of any sport undertaken in nature. Nature out here has its own rhythms, which we understand only imperfectly, if at all. In any case, the BLM is monitoring the dunes, logging on everyone's theories, and scratching its head over how to handle a complaint about an event for which it has just issued a three-year permit to be held each year in the same place on the playa so it can monitor the effects.

In the meantime, the Burning Man organization has been developing burn shields so the Man and other conflagrations don't scorch the alkali surface even temporarily. They've dramatically increased the number of portable toilets during the event in order to forestall human waste making it into the dust. The Earth Guardians have a booth promoting environmentally sound practices, and all of us spend a fair portion of our time while walking around with our eyes on the ground and picking up whatever fugitive scraps we see, which are surprisingly few, given our throwaway camping culture.

By the time I've thoroughly examined the weather, which looks as if it's clearing, and taken notes in the relatively dust-free passenger seat of the van (the driver's seat being inaccessible from the outside because the parachute is partially anchored over it), Walter has cooked up the sausage with scrambled eggs, hash browns, and bread toasted in a skillet. After serving everyone the late breakfast, he's already thinking about lunch. The guy can eat more than any three people I know. Personally, I'm ready to visit the café on the edge of the center ring, and maybe see if I can find my official contact, Jim Graham, at the Media Mecca tent.

After the dishes are cleaned up and the camp more or less secured against marauding dust, we all take off in different directions. We've only been here since late yesterday afternoon and are anxious to see the place during daylight. Laurel and Walter will probably go out to where David Best, a friend and artist from Petaluma in Sonoma County, has been constructing a large wooden house during the last week. Before the fatal motorcycle accident, Michael Hefflin had worked in Best's shop, and David had adopted the genial, footloose guy as an informal son. Originally planning just to make an empty house as a sculpture to be burned down on Friday night, now it's becoming something of a shrine to Michael, and Laurel and Walter are anxious to see it. Tarn and Jonah wander off as well, and I head toward the city center to register as a member of the media, something I rarely do when writing on location, but which is required here.

My route takes me up the axial boulevard that runs from the entrance of the city to the Man himself, a thoroughfare that bisects the great sweeping arcs of streets named after body parts. The walk into Center Camp from the perimeter of the encampment, where we've lodged ourselves near the rambling and profoundly graffitied Department of Public Works compound, takes about twenty minutes. The sun has come out, and as quickly as the day warms up, off come the clothes. Guys are walking around with nothing on but penis sheaths, while some women sport shaved and painted pudenda. On the other hand, several people on bicycles pass me wearing suits and ties.

The central core of the city is devoted to the Man and the larger art projects, a circle of open playa many acres in extent where numerous pyrotechnic setups are separated by hundreds of yards for safety's sake. Surrounding the huge arena in a semicircle, the innermost ring of the city is defined by theme camps featuring entertainments from claustrophobic fabric mazes encouraging anonymous bodily contact with other participants, to elaborate performances projected on outsized screens. The next ring out includes all the practicalities, such as a compact but fully functional garage servicing bicycles, a large first-aid tent, an FM radio station, and the media lounge area.

I don't see Jim Graham, with whom I've been communicating via e-mail for several months, but do find someone to check in with, a woman with a binder of release forms for authorized media people to sign. Sprawled on several couches in various stages of alertness are writers, camera crews, sound technicians, and reporters. The BBC is here, both the *New York Times* and *Los Angeles Times*, a crew from *National Geographic*, and dozens of others from the roughly 150 media outlets in attendance. Not everyone gets approved as media—a rave magazine wanting to do a story, for instance, was denied official access, since the Burning Man organization doesn't want to promote the false idea that the festival is an Ecstasy-fueled all-night dance party. And anyone found taking photographs without authorization is summarily ejected from the city. Privacy is a major concern from two standpoints. First, people are letting go here, which is the point, and although voyeurism is welcomed, most of us would prefer not to have our exuberant pictures in the hometown daily. Second, it's a matter of principle: the event and its contents are not for sale. You can buy a cup of coffee here, and a bag of ice, but that's it. All other transactions, whether they're for a pinch of salt, fixing a flat tire, or a massage are based on a gift economy.

While I'm shamelessly wandering around the Media Mecca in order to eavesdrop on my colleagues, a short, stout, somewhat excitable young man strides in asking "Where are the costumes?"—a request the staff easily accommodates. The organizers encourage media people to get involved, to be participants even as they're documenting the proceedings. In furnishing the requisite props, they actually help the cynics among us get more into the spirit of things. Personally, I'm happy to be clad in hiking shorts and a khaki shirt, though I've been teased while walking around for carrying a pad and pen.

One thing the organizers do well is give good meteorological advice, the collective well-being of the city dependent on preparation for various states of weather. The media handlers are letting everyone know that a vigorous windstorm is on its way, so I head back to camp. First I detour, however, over to the tented public café, which encloses several performance stages, the coffee stand (which has a long line in front of it), and any number of seating arrangements. Rugs are set out on the dirt, couches are strewn almost but not quite haphazardly about, and potted bamboo screens off little corners here and there. Rick's Bar in *Casablanca* has finally met, quite deliberately, the famous bar scene from *Star Wars*.

An acoustic guitarist is giving a solo performance at one end while a drum circle surrounded by dancers thumps rhythmically away at the other. The tent is so large, and the crowd just dense enough, that the two don't conflict. A woman dressed in nothing but thin black leather straps leads a man on a leash, his legs encased in insectoidal metal extensions so that he walks on hands and knees, but suspended several feet above the floor. A deeply tanned guy in his seventies sits nude nearby chatting with a man in a burnoose and long robes. The aesthetic overall is early-nineteenth-century Orientalism, that English colonial construct brought back from around the Empire and fed to London audiences avid for titillating evidence of the Other. I take Burning Man seriously enough as an expression of our public unconscious to wonder if this isn't evidence that America is girding itself for a serious co-option of the Islamic world. If we can't overthrow their leaders, maybe we'll conquer them by adopting their dress code.

The rest of the day I spend in our camp, mostly in the van after the prophesied windstorms arrive, fifty-mile-an-hour gusts rocking the van back and forth on its springs. We've cut strategic holes in the parachute to let the wind and alkali blow through, but it's still a surprise to see by dinnertime that the camp chairs, tables, stoves, and food boxes remain in place, if filled with dust. Walter and Laurel have returned from working on David's house with an invitation for us to join him that evening for some kind of celebration, but first we do some serious and well-vintaged rehydration along with pasta and salad. Only then do we head out for a nighttime tour.

Last night, we'd taken a long reconnaissance around the inner ring of the city, and I'm reminded this evening how different the place is once the sun sets. During the day, everything exterior is buttoned down and relatively colorless, coated with dust and bleached out by bright sun. Now lanterns, neon tubing, propane torches, and kerosene-soaked balls of rags are burning everywhere. Huge fireballs rise into the air with a *Whump!* and the rank odor of hydrocarbons wafts about. All I can compare it to is as if the visitors thronging the Las Vegas Strip one night had climbed up into the lights and brought them down onto the street to play with them.

It's a poor analogy, and I give up any pretension of analysis in order to enjoy myself. This turns out to be the right move. Reaching David Best's elaborate camp, made up of several portable storage structures arrayed in a star pattern around a tented courtyard, we find ourselves being guided onto his "Bar Car," a Jeep that's been chopped, had a full bar and a small dance floor welded onto it, and is about to take off for a tour of the central playa.

For the next couple of hours, we glide along in the dark, the driver, whose head is on level with everyone else's feet, taking an occasional bearing off brightly lit art projects here and there around the city's circular promenade. Walter keeps him supplied with drinks, while Tarn and Jonah stand with Laurel on the port side, talking and smoking. Mary Morelli, a pattern designer with the Levi Corporation in San Francisco who shares the front railing with me, compares the distant semicircle of lights to the Long Island shoreline, an image perfectly suited to sailing on a party barge across the playa.

Schools of bicycles ride up to and circle us, the riders and their machines outlined with glow sticks—flexible cold chemical tubes emitting red, green, or blue neonlike light—as if we're on a submersible surrounded by the self-illuminating fish of the bathymetric ocean. Occasionally one of the riders leaps onto the Bar Car for a minute or two for a drink, then gaily departs off the back into the dark. The ride is both a giddy frolic and profoundly lovely, a joyride and a procession for Michael, who can't be with us. One can't help but feel that much more of life should be conducted in such a fashion.

At midnight, we return to David's camp, where we abandon ship and decide to go examine one of the lasers projecting light over the playa. Several towers placed hundreds of yards apart trace an outstretched schematic of the Burning Man each night, the body as map beamed out for miles over the city, bright green argon-powered lines etching the night thirty feet over our heads. The laser we walk to tonight, however, is throwing up a sheet of light that weaves intricate and glittering patterns in the dust that dances in the air. It's mesmerizing, like so many of the light shows here, and even though we're getting cold, it's with reluctance that we return to camp.

FRIDAY, SEPTEMBER 2

The next morning I rise around eight, make coffee, and enjoy a clear sky and the morning sun, neither of which is going to stick around for much of the day. Once again the west is hosting bands of cloud, but today they're much thicker in girth. We're going to have not only wind but a heavier rain, I think.

By ten, most everyone is up and ready for a light breakfast. We're going over to a friend's for a gourmet salmon barbecue later in the afternoon, and we need just enough carbos for now to counteract the mild excesses of cabernet the night before. This morning Walter cooks, I wash, Laurel dries, Tarn and Jonah smoke. We rotate duties each day, though Walter is definitely and to our bliss doing most of the cooking. Afterward, everyone wanders off to check out art projects or talk to friends, leaving me alone to read and write.

It's a leisurely morning, the water trucks going by at regular intervals. I listen to two of the forty-one FM and AM radio stations set up for the week, one featuring nonstop Burning Man City news, including a confirmation that precipitation is forecast. The other station features a mix of contemporary music, some of which I know, most of which I don't, and all of it better than what I'd find on the best stations in Los Angeles, save perhaps KCRW.

Twice during the morning, lumbering prop-driven C-130 cargo planes, presumably out of the Fallon Naval Air Station or from the Air National Guard based in Reno, fly overhead at a moderately low altitude. Binoculars show them to be from more than one branch of the services, so I'm not sure where they're originating, but they're outside the approved Military Operations Area and what they're doing is semilegal at best, though hardly surprising. Officials in the BLM's Winnemucca Field Office who are responsible for governing the Black Rock and issuing permits to Burning Man have actually witnessed troops being dropped on the playa north of the city in other years, perhaps using it as a mock enemy encampment to be infiltrated. Navy SEALS, U.S. Army Special Forces—all the elite groups use the desert for such exercises, and we must make a tempting and entertaining target.

While I've been taking notes, the wind has been stealthily gaining strength, and by two o'clock everyone has returned to rendezvous for the salmon bake, which is a fifteen-minute walk along the outside circle of the city. Small planes are landing and taking off from the dirt runway that is the temporary airport, even though the wind is occasionally blowing hard enough to push bicycle riders northward without their having to peddle.

Our fashionably late luncheon turns out to be a laid-back affair with an astonishing amount of fish and wine set out inside a tent. The meal is punctuated by another flyby of a cargo plane, a dust storm violent enough to unanchor part of our host's large geodesic dome, a parade of DPW vehicles (one of which every minute or so launches an alarmingly large jet of burning gas into the air), and three hundred women riding by bare-breasted on bicycles, a perennial Burning Man favorite. We stagger home afterward during a break in the turbulent clouds of dust rolling periodically through the city, producing short-lived whiteouts, and relax in preparation for a long night. A light shower passes through about five o'clock, coating the windows of the van with mud so thick that I have to turn on the windshield wipers to regain enough daylight so I can keep writing.

A primary objective for me today is to visit David Best's sculpture in order to see it before it burns, so Jonah takes me there just before twilight. As we strike out across the interior playa, what at first appears no larger than a small box on the desert floor soon grows into a structure nearly three stories tall. Assembled out of scrap lumber ranging from an eighth-inch to a half-inch thick, the building resembles an elaborate Hindu temple, intricate in a thousand ways yet airy, its dim interior pierced with evening light. We squeeze through a gap in the back wall and find ourselves circling around an altar with a small framed picture of Michael on it. Around us, dozens of people are moving quietly and slowly, almost reverentially.

David is at the front door, a compact man with a short white beard handing out small pieces of leftover wood. "If you lost someone you love," he's telling two young women, "write down their name or something about them, and leave it on the altar. Then come back at midnight and we'll burn it all together." He waves them deeper inside, an Italian journalist and her assistant next in line and obviously confused by what he's saying.

"This is wonderful," she exclaims, gesturing around her. "Can we come back . . . ah, umm . . . tomorrow to film it?"

"No, no, we're going to burn it tonight," he replies, offering her a piece of wood. This causes deep consternation. She searches for words: "But how can you . . . destroy this . . . it is so beautiful!"

David seeks valiantly to explain, the woman sending out her assistant to bring in the cameraman, none of them speaking very good English. We leave David to cope and walk out the front for another view. Outside, hundreds of people are coming up to and going away from the piece. As David will later confirm, dozens of rumors about it are circulating.

"Yeah, he made every piece beforehand and numbered 'em all. Took him six months, and then he reassembled it up here."

"Spielberg's gonna come watch this thing burn!"

"Nah, they're not really burning it. Coppola commissioned it, and he's sending a cargo 'copter to come pick it up. It's gonna sit in front of his winery."

Some of the rumors, David confesses, were started by none other than himself. One year he brought a taxidermied horse to immolate at Burning Man, and a rumor started that it had been the stand-in for Anthony Quinn's steed in the film *Lawrence of Arabia*. Then there was the stuffed dog he brought that people speculated was Old Yeller's stand-in from the movie of the same name, a tale he didn't bother to contradict. Born in 1945 and educated at the San Francisco Art Institute, Best has always found death and religion to be strong catalysts for his work, which he describes as being "found-object junk sculpture." It's a genre in which humor balances the more somber aspects of art.

Jonah and I mostly ignore the crowd and turn to observe the front of the house, which is now illuminated with spotlights. I finger the thin piece of hobby wood that David's given me. The load-bearing skeleton of the structure appears to be simple, a foursquare construct of two-by-fours with a ground floor and a second level open to the sky where people are still hammering. But its distinctive curlicues are complicated, produced by David sawing up wood that he salvages from other places where it's already been cut and left behind as scrap. The pieces are juxtaposed on the house in such a way as to make it appear almost as if gargoyles are perched on the corners. A vague organic morphism suffuses the walls, a perception that floats in and out of focus as your vision and imagination constantly trade places. The effect is akin to what some stained-glass windows in cathedrals, as well as some abstract artworks, are supposed to do: cut apart and then reassemble the world into nonrepresentational but evocative shapes that free the mind for contemplation.

It occurs to me a little later in camp, while chasing down a light snack with vodka martinis, that being at Burning Man is itself like taking a cruise on a luxury liner, David's Bar Car an apt image for the occasion. The accommodations this week are a little more vernacular, but basically you eat and stroll from one entertainment to another, and then eat again. If it weren't for the amount of walking we're doing every day, we'd actually gain weight out here, although in years when it's hot on the playa, most people find themselves consuming only about half their usual amount of calories, the body simply refusing to hold much appetite for anything but liquids.

In any case, the one time I took an ocean cruise, I felt guilty for days on end about our conspicuous consumption while crossing such a sublime space as the Pacific. I'm experiencing a twinge of that now, caused by the transition from contemplating David's sculpture, and Michael's death, to the sybaritic snack. Tarn, experiencing this in his own way, has no appetite.

By eleven-thirty we're back in front of the house, around which have collected several thousand people, many of whom know that this is a memorial event for a dead friend of the sculptor. For the moment, the wind and intermittent showers have ceased, and luckily, since otherwise the burn would have to be postponed until tomorrow night, which would create a clear conflict with the big burning of the Man.

Laurel, Jonah, and Walter stand at the front of the crowd. I hover behind them, not wanting to intrude. Tarn's elsewhere in the great milling circumference, not particularly desirous of company for the moment. David, accompanied by a fireman in his heavy coat, and a couple of crew members go in and out of the building repeatedly, soaking diesel fuel into strategic places for the public immolation of sorrow and loss. Laurel alternately rests her head on Walter's shoulder and hugs Jonah.

By midnight, the crowd is getting restless, and despite the solemnity of the event (or at least our perception of such), begins to chant

"Bu-u-urn it! Bu-u-urn it! Bu-u-urn it!" I'm put off a bit by such a vocal demand, but David has taken the attitude that the more people who inquire if this is his artwork, the more it belongs to them, not him. It's appropriate, then, that at a quarter after the hour, a small flame appears in front of and beneath the altar, where it glows cheerfully for some minutes but refuses to spread. One of David's crew sneaks in a side door and pours more flammables, then lights a second fire, which slowly joins with the first, the altar now beginning to smoke. Someone in the crowd throws a lit firework toward the house, an extremely unwise gesture that makes the crowd uneasy.

When the front of the house goes, at about twelve-thirty, it goes quickly, the flames shooting up ten, twenty, then thirty feet, the heat suddenly so intense that everyone moves backward with alacrity. Fireworks embedded in the top of the house go off and huge clouds of sparks drift over us. We stop moving. As the fire eats deeper into the house and the initial blast of heat passes, the crowd pushes slowly forward again. A light drizzle is falling now, rain glowing in white streaks around what resolves into the giant and mostly intact ember of a house.

How often, I ask myself, can you watch a house burn with pleasure? This virtual funeral pyre is an exquisite icon standing free in the air, and as its timbers slowly collapse, it seems to take so much sadness with it. Laurel will write me later to say that the burning was a more satisfactory ritual for her than the actual preparing and throwing of Michael's ashes into the sea, and to wonder if the fascination and fear we feel before a fire isn't related to how we consider death, a thought with which the artist would probably agree.

We retire to David's compound, leaving the crowd behind to warm themselves around the coals. While Jonah and David open a bottle of wine and pass out cigars, the rain returns in earnest. I stand by myself to one side, lost in the heavy drumming of a desert downpour as they share toasts. When everyone sits down in a circle to pass around the wine and tell stories about Michael, they invite me to join them.

"This is something new for Burning Man," the sculptor states quietly. He's exhausted, but working up a second wind. "This wasn't just a piece of decoration to burn, and it wasn't something just for us. The more people put messages into it, the more it became a work of art. This was for everyone, it was empty until they filled it, and this is what Burning Man is going to have to live up to in the future."

I have no illusions about really being part of this tightly knit group of friends, or of being as integral a part of the Burning Man community as David, but I don't believe he's overstating the case when he calls the house "a temple." Too many people in the crowd had been talking about the scraps they'd written on and left in the fire, too many people were telling stories about family members no longer with them and crying. David's not boasting about what he's done, just saying that the house has performed more than one function, added a deeper, more private, and unforeseen layer to people's experience here. What more could an artist aspire toward?

The wake goes on and on, and I rise to leave while there's a break in the rain. David is offering to cook everyone omelets, but I'm so tired I can hardly see. I hand him a book of poems that I've brought as a gift to thank him for so generously including me, then start the walk back to our camp. It's a hellacious teeth-chattering march. The hard-packed surface of the playa has turned to mud that builds up underneath my shoes until three inches thick, then falls off, first from one shoe, then the other, so I'm always walking lopsided. I consider crawling into someone else's camp to beg for warmth, but I've suffered playa mud before and press on. Several people are carrying bicycles over their shoulders, the tires immobilized by mud packed tight up into the fenders.

I crawl into my bag at three-thirty in the morning, rouse briefly when the others come home a little later, then awaken twice more to rain tat-tattering away on our tents and the parachute, but I have no trouble falling back each time into a long and uncomplicated sleep.

After a late brunch the next morning, I saunter back toward the Media Mecca. A long line of cars is leaving the city, reportedly a thousand campers fleeing the scene before the Man has even burned. Their tents have blown out, or they didn't bring enough warm clothes, or it's all just too much trouble. But this is exactly what defines the Black Rock Desert, cycles of sun and wind and rain relentlessly burnishing the floor of the basin down to a mirror upon which we watch ourselves walk. I'm delighted for those Burners who will stay. They're not seeing this place as a static stage but as a process through which we're living, which is what landscape is all about.

This time I do locate Jim Graham, who, when I introduce myself, says, "Oh, yeah, you're the guy who's been walking around the playas for the last year. It's great you're here."

I find myself unexpectedly flattered to be identified with the landform, which not everyone would pick as their totemic landscape, and we have a quick conversation about how the event is going, much of which centers around the weather. We're interrupted by an older gentleman on a bicycle demanding to know who authorized a camera crew to set up near the Man, thus blocking off a sliver out of what would otherwise be an uninterrupted 360° view. Jim, a tall man with a comfortable waistline and a steady stance on the ground, is mild and unflappable in return. "We did. It's a webcast crew that will uplink a live video of the burn."

The man sputters in protest, incredulous that the Burning Man organization could be so crass and commercial as to allow such a thing. He rides off shaking his beard, muttering about the event not being like it used to. Jim smiles. This is a familiar plaint, but although I find the event much different from the one in 1992, it seems no more commercial now than when Misrach and Goin were documenting the event with still and video cameras. The photo agreement, which anyone making professional images at the event must sign, stipulates in great detail how they may be used, and that 10 percent of all proceeds must come back to the organization to help with operating expenses, grants to artists working on the playa, and so forth.

I exit the tent when it's obvious that Jim needs to cope with messages over his walkie-talkie and wander back to camp via some streets I haven't yet explored. Although some Burners are living out of backpacking tents or the bland interiors of rented RVs, our setup is pretty utilitarian compared to others. A white picket fence has been erected around one place, complete with a green plastic lawn in parody of suburbia. Signs outside other miniature environments advertise experiments in everything from black lights to sexual voyeurism.

Later in the afternoon, I return with Tarn to hang out in the café, listen to music, and watch people. Beyond the aforementioned tendencies to dress like a refugee from an Arabic *Star Wars*, an aesthetic wisely derived from cultures much more experienced in desert living than ours, no law of averages is apparent here, the dominant aesthetic of personal appearance being a null set. Lots of tattoos and body piercings, yes, but also relatively clean-cut types like me in hiking clothes. Dogs are discouraged from attending, since they're relatively difficult to pick up after, but ferrets are in evidence, heads popping out of sleeves. I have no doubt that somewhere in the city a pet snake or two is coiled up in a basket.

Tarn stretches out on a rug and naps, while next to us a young guy recites his poetry from memory. No one is drinking publicly or consuming drugs, that being left to the privacy of each camp, a carefully negotiated understanding between the organizers and law-enforcement officials that's mostly held up during the week. As a result, plenty of people are in a steady state of chemical alteration, but there's no menace in the air. No matter where I've walked or at what time of night, this is the safest I've felt in a city since working as a trekking guide out of Kathmandu in the mid-1970s.

It's already after eight o'clock when we head out from camp to the Man himself, and by the time we enter the interior playa, we see that the figure outlined in magenta and blue neon is already burning. Yesterday, people were climbing atop the eight levels of hay baloo —which elevated the Man enough above the surface so that he was visible throughout the city—and having their pictures taken while standing between the legs, like tourists posing with a national monument. Now his stance is filled with fire, and only one arm is left upright, so fast are the flames climbing up the fifty-foot-tall wooden sculpture. We skirt to the right to avoid the heaviest crowding and end up climbing ten feet up a metal "Rib Cage–Bird Cage" sculpture we'd visited the first night.

The vantage point is a good one, and as the Man is reduced to a glowing heap, I'm surprised to see how different the reaction of this crowd is to the one eight years earlier. No impromptu mass movement around the bonfire occurs; there are just too many people, and it becomes obvious that Burning Man is no longer about the center of the event, but the periphery.

Before we can climb down, a man below us starts playing a calliope that shoots flaming propane out of its vertical tubes instead of notes, an event that has its own crowd of hundreds. Careful to keep track of one another as we depart, we next visit the "Thunderdome," a huge geodesic jungle gym inside which fire-slingers twirl kerosene-soaked balls on short ropes and a man in black exhales flames from his mouth. Dozens of people cling all over the metal structure watching the action. Around midnight, we witness a thirty-foot-high penis made of lathe and chicken wire coated with playa mud slowly melt from intense fire drafting up its shaft. A large van parks nearby, upon the roof of which are positioned two enormous Tesla coils, which have apparently been liberated from the laboratory of Dr. Frankenstein. Standing between them and dressed in an insulated suit, Dr. Megavolt draws forth crackling bolts of lightning, the thick writhing snakes of blue electricity incinerating objects tossed up to him by spectators.

I leave Tarn and the others to contemplate what must be at least two dozen kinds of up-close and personal pyrotechnics, ranging from the almost-cosmic power of Megavolt to people with candles lit atop their heads, the wax dripping down about them. It's more than I can absorb in one night, and I'm wishing we'd gotten here a couple of days earlier and wondering if we should come back next year.

Stories are told about how difficult it can be to leave the playa, and we're talking traffic jam here, not just emotional attachment. The stream of cars passing in front of us never seems to come to a halt. Individual vehicles sometimes break out of line so people can deposit spare food and water for the Department of Public Works personnel, who will be out here cleaning up until October 2nd, the BLM deadline by which the playa must be restored as closely as possible to its original condition. Otherwise, it's an orderly exodus, and by the time we're packed up and ready to leave in early afternoon, there's no delay in getting out the gates. Tarn and I wave goodbye to Jonah, Walter, and Laurel, who turn left for Reno and the interstate back to the Bay Area. We head the other way, over to the Smoke Creek and Michael Moore's place for a shower, dinner, and a night's rest before driving up to Portland.

Michael and Linda have had a hectic summer, as it turns out, closing the deal on a building in Benicia, while Linda negotiated with representatives from a major department store for a large sculpture she'll build for their new downtown-San Francisco location. Although they've made the decision that the large room in the house is to be a living room and not a studio, the seventy-six watercolors Mike's painted this summer are pinned up in a grid on the high walls, and some of the thirteen larger acrylics he also completed are propped up along another. Many, many mirages on the Black Rock were done from memory while he was in Colorado, their doubled horizons hovering in that peculiar indeterminate space created by temperature discontinuities above the playa. "In order to depict particles suspended in dry air," Linda notes of his technique, "you actually use more water in the paint." Ever the teacher as well as the artist, she enjoys the mild irony.

I look at the mirages, those miracles of visual inversion that hover temporarily two or three miles out in front of us, and think about the ephemerality of Burning Man, about how the playas of the West form and reform their surfaces each year, about the burning of David's house that became a sculpture and then a temple—and then disappeared. I lean back on the couch facing the small paintings and daydream about Michael Heizer's *Nine Nevada Depressions,* all of which have long since filled in, and the geoglyphs of the Indians, which are being picked apart by teenagers to be reformed as new messages.

The playas are equally about absence and presence, a visual field that almost demands that we recreate ourselves because out there, on the largest, flattest, and clearest places on land that we can find, there's no illusion of permanence, hence no reason to not do so. Nowhere else can we see the ground upon which we stand be swept so clean. It may take a while—there are still shell casings sitting out on the surface at the far north end of the Black Rock playa where fighter planes emptied machine-gun clips at targets during World War II—but the silts continue to accumulate each year, and the waters come and go, smoothing out the relics and the memories. Eventually, the old munitions will sink into the earth along with everything else, just as the continent itself will someday be subsumed into the earth's mantle by larger tectonic forces.

And if the earth recreates itself on a regular basis, it would seem there might be reason for us to do so as well.

Rediscovery

An Afterword

Two weeks after Burning Man and I'm already back on the Black Rock, this time with the photographer Mark Klett to work on a small collaborative book about the playa for the University of Arizona Press. A series of prose and photographic meditations, it will offer us a chance to work beyond the confines of our trips taken with the Third View team each summer, which are a continuation of the Rephotographic Survey Project done by Mark and others in the 1970s. That "Second View" project retraced work done by the nineteenth-century exploration photographers a hundred years earlier; the Third View is exactly that, a third look, this time done after an interval of only twenty years. Mark works as the principal photographer for the team, which includes several other artists and myself as the writer of the field notes.

In contrast, then, to the more clearly defined summer work, this is an opportunity to investigate a place where it's only the terrain that's been predetermined and not specific vantage points for photographs and text. We've convinced Alvin McLane, given his intimate knowledge of both the terrain and the history of the Black Rock, to join us for three of the four days we'll spend out here.

We roll through Gerlach early on a Sunday evening and drive up along the western edge of the playa looking for a small draw with a stream and some sheltering cottonwoods where Alvin and I have camped before. Turning off on the dirt road, we're soon stopped by a new fence erected by a corporation, Bright-Holland, the name of which none of us recognizes. Fuming, we backtrack to a more exposed site, one with a trashed-out fire ring but that's still open to the public. Our spirits recover somewhat over dinner as we watch the headlights of about fifty motorcycles advancing in a line up the far side of the playa, their motive a mystery. While a huge harvest moon is rising, fireworks explode silently in the sky to the east, and we later learn that the riders were conducting a wake for a fallen comrade.

The next day, we drive out north in Alvin's Jeep across the flats to the Black Rock itself, the four-hundred-foot-high outcropping of dark sedimentary and volcanic rocks that was used as a landmark by every explorer and emigrant coming through since Frémont was the first Euro-American to cross the playa. Located about eighteen miles from the Burning Man camp, it had been just far enough away that we couldn't see it, and I had felt peculiar about being in the middle of the playa without that specific reference point.

Mark rides up front for his first trip across the playa, a 70-mph drive along the centermost of the three semi-established roads that cross the desert and are usable only in the summer and fall. Off to our right in the distance are two portable toilets, a forklift, and what appears to be a group of people standing in a line on the desert. It's the forty-person cleanup crew from Burning Man working a grid, cleaning up the site of the city block-by-block. This year the BLM will test random transects within the former city limits, as well as outside it. They'll take soil samples from each, compare the contents, and even weigh them to determine the residual impacts of the event. It looks like Will Roger, the head of the Burning Man Department of Public Works who has moved to Gerlach to be in charge of the site full time, is taking the cleanup successfully to a new level of obsession.

Soon we're at the far edge of the playa, defined here by a maze formed of phreatophyte mounds. These formations, generally two or three feet high, are formed by windblown sand collecting around the base of salt-tolerant plants, which make them grow just a little taller each year, and the mounds to accumulate just a bit higher. The process eventually places the plants on such a high pedestal that their roots can no longer reach water, whereupon they die and the mounds slowly disintegrate back down to ground level. Remnants of old phreatophyte mounds are found even fairly far out on the playa, bespeaking a variable climate.

Before wending our way through the sandy humps, we stop to photograph detritus on the playa floor, which over the next several days will include broken beer bottles, a moccasin, the lower jaw of a coyote, miscellaneous small scraps of lumber and white plastic pipes, golf tees, the remnants of hobby-rocket launch pads, and nine different caliber shell casings ranging from petite .22 shells to 20-mm shells almost twice the size of my forefinger. The prehistoric lithic scatter is very light, but mixed in with the munitions we find chips of worked chert, quartz, and jasper.

This morning, Mark concentrates on a broken amber beer bottle lying near a .50-caliber shell, the two artifacts a visual metaphor for the shift in usage from the military to recreational, the same change in usage Matt Coolidge and I witnessed while touring through the Mojave playas this last spring. Mark also pokes gingerly around a live .50-caliber round from the late 1940s that rests not far from the beer bottle. Given the hundreds of shell casings and machine-gun clips that we find half-buried in the alkali, which date from World War II onward through the 1950s, I suspect that the scavengers from Slab City would feel right at home here.

After Alvin guides us around the Black Rock Spring, some of the old emigrant trail and, a few miles to the north, the even-hotter Double Hot Springs, we feel like we need more time at this end of the west arm of the desert and should come back to camp under the Black Rock tonight. Returning across the playa to collect the rented van that I've driven up from Los Angeles, and which we've left at Bruno's Restaurant in Gerlach, we're stopped by a search-and-rescue unit looking for a downed motorcyclist. We haven't seen any riders since early this morning, when two of them were racing up the flat, and are dismayed at how invisible a motorcycle would be out here to a search unit. As we enter town, a helicopter goes by, either to help locate the bikes or to extract someone.

Once again we drive out over the playa, and I parallel the Jeep's course in the van. Because there's nothing on the surface that your eyes can focus on, concentration drifts. My quite-literal spaciness is rudely interrupted as I radically readjust the front-end alignment, inadvertently discovering those little dunes mentioned earlier, the "playa serpents." Although both a bit wobblier after the high-speed encounter, the van and I are essentially fine, and we make it back to the base of the rock in forty-five minutes. At thirty miles north of Gerlach, hence almost three times farther out than when at Burning Man and at the juncture of the east and west arms of the desert, we're ideally poised for Mark to make a panorama in the morning.

Although it's relatively easy to photograph the edges of the playa, as well as to make closeups of things on its surface—both situations providing scale and naturally occurring frames for the views—capturing the actual expanse of the playa will be a challenge that perhaps only several shots stitched together can handle. Egloffstein, of course, faced the same dilemma when making his panorama, done above the southern end of the playa in 1854. Mark will adopt a similar strategy, climbing partway up the Black Rock in order to obtain a perspective that can encompass a large area and will allow him to rotate the camera through a series of shots.

For the next two days, we explore both arms of the playa and the range in between. Alvin patiently traces out the Applegate-Lassen Cutoff, taking us to where the emigrants would have had their first view of the playa up by Rabbit Hole Spring. We crisscross the basin a dozen times or more, at one point Mark taping binoculars to his camera so he can photograph mirages and the vehicles that occasionally arise out of them. The results on Polaroid film are reminiscent of Michael Moore's paintings, which Mark hasn't yet seen. Although we pass and are passed by other vehicles on the playa, mostly ranchers coming out of Gerlach and members of the Burning Man cleanup crew, we only talk to one person while out of town, a German tourist in a rented suv who's looking for hot springs.

One of the most cherished myths about the Black Rock playa—as it is on any large stretch of flat land, including the Central Valley of California and the Great Plains—is that you can see the curvature of the earth while standing out on it. Unfortunately, this is a physical impossibility, given the lack of sufficient elevation on any of those places.

While photographing, we do confirm that the playa does, indeed, seem to swell in the middle, but this has more to do with the nature of its subsurface than global geometry. The playa collects runoff from about 2,600 square miles, according to Barbara Bilbo, a geomorphologist writing about the Black Rock Desert, and the subsequent saturation of thousands of feet of silts and clay beds that underlie the playa causes the swelling in the center, hence the apparent curvature.

Alvin departs for Reno on Tuesday after lunch, and that night Mark and I end up in the Quinn River Sink, where the intermittent river debouches in wet years, and which I consider the most mysterious part of the playa. It's shown on some maps as a dangerous area in which to travel because of its unpredictable conditions and precipitous runoff channels. Even during the summer, the sub-basin can hold enough water just under the surface to trap unwary tourists, and the numerous channels are a hazard unexpected by most drivers who have been running freely on the flats.

Where we camp, however, is an almost perfectly level surface. Even the surrounding mountains are only a distant ring of silhouette as the sun sets, and it's now that we can at least infer the curvature of the earth, but only in the slight arc of its shadow, the terminator, rising into the eastern sky just ahead of the deeper darkness of the night.

The only light on the ground that's visible is a very faint one to the south, perhaps a camp lantern, and we are even out of range of the glow cast by Reno some 140 miles to the south, which otherwise pollutes the night sky in parts of northwestern Nevada. The densest part of the Milky Way, the Cygnus region, is straight overhead, and we walk away from camp with our heads tilted back, not having to watch the ground. It's a liberated feeling, and we hold out our arms parallel to the equator of the galaxy and spin once, twice, then stop. Without any ground-based reference points, the experience is so deeply dizzying that we have trouble standing.

Staying up until almost eleven o'clock to watch a half-moon rise through narrow clouds, we examine its great dusty plains through

Mark Klett, *image of mirage.* Reproduced with the permission of Mark Klett

binoculars. As yet another kind of desert, it also has been a receptacle for human imagination, providing a home for mythological gods and monsters, utopian sci-fi societies, and a base for aliens—the very inhabitants still proposed for the playas on earth.

We want to sleep out in the open this last night on the desert but reluctantly opt for tents to avoid the small scorpions that have come out in the dark to mate, there being enough moisture in this far end of the playa to sustain them. Even so, it's a wonderful night for sleeping, more quiet than any other I can remember, and it's just cold enough that I zip up my sleeping bag for the first time since last fall a year ago.

The next morning, after the daily sunrise photography ritual, breakfast, and some drive-by beachcombing for desert detritus, Mark deploys his pocket transit, a Brunton compass from his days as a field geologist with the USGS, to survey one of the drops from the east arm, which he measures at more than six and a half feet high. It's actually an old spit formed as part of the last shoreline that Lake Lahontan created about six thousand years ago. Given that the entire Black Rock playa varies less than five feet over most of its length, that's an impressive variation, and definitely a feature you wouldn't want to drive over without looking where you're going.

Jim Graham has sent me Global Positioning System (GPS) coordinates for the site of the Burning Man figure ("plus or minus three feet"), and we continue our survey work by plotting our way over to the site of the big burn. Out in the center of the playa, Mark doesn't even bother to look where he's driving, but just watches the screen of his handheld GPS unit as he keeps his other hand on the wheel to make course adjustments. We park at the coordinates, get out, hike around in widening circles, and find nothing but a single pink feather and a half-dozen metal spacers the size of dimes. Even these will disappear when the cleanup crew, which is doing its line dance in the distance over the city grid, gets here next week. We don't bother to look for the site of David Best's house; in addition to torching it atop one of the approved burn mats, thus leaving no scorch marks, he's actually vacuumed the entire site. The BLM tried to examine where he'd built his project but couldn't find the spot, so thoroughly had all traces been removed.

Before heading into town, where we'll finish our visit by attending a BLM public-comment meeting on its new management proposal for the Black Rock, we head over to Trego Hot Springs for a bath. The springs, which have replaced Fly Geyser as a bathing spot for Burners since it was closed by the ominously widespread Bright-Holland Corporation, are located within a few yards of the train tracks. We conclude that the train engineers must be delighted when they roar by at 70 mph and catch glimpses of nude crowds walking around the banks on Labor Day Weekend. Even though the cleanup crew is still using this as a spot to relax sore muscles, today we're alone. It feels good to bathe, yet as always I regret washing off the alkali dust, which I've come to regard as a badge of time on the playa. No doubt the people we'll see tonight will appreciate it, however.

When we pull into Bruno's for dinner, five BLM trucks are parked around the building; apparently the troops are out in force tonight. A little after 7 P.M., we're all in the Gerlach Community Center, Mark and I taking a seat in back. Mike Bilbo from the BLM is there, along with his boss, Field Manager Terry Reed, and so is Burning Man's Will Roger with several of his cleanup crew in tow. Of the forty people present, seven are BLM representatives. Most of the public who are here to comment on the government's management plan are local business people and ranchers, and many clutch copies of the yellow-jacketed inch-and-a-quarter-thick document.

What is to be done with the Black Rock has long been a difficult question for locals, visitors, and various levels of government. In July 1967, for instance, the Reno newspapers reported that San Francisco was considering the Black Rock as the site for a landfill to accept 1,500 tons of garbage daily, a plan that was later dropped because it wasn't cost effective. At least that's not an option on the table tonight, but competition between development and recreational use is still the primary issue, and the public is being asked to comment on three alternatives for how they will experience the playa in the future.

The BLM's presentation boils down roughly to this. The "No Action Alternative" leaves things the way they are, except for expanding the existing environmental study area up by Soldier Meadows at the far north end of the west arm. That would put 35,000 acres off limits to oil, gas, and mineral development, versus 3,500, but leave pretty much intact the ability of anyone to roam anywhere else.

"Alternative 1," which the agency prefers, would start to place limits on "camping, access, off-highway vehicle use, and large-scale recreation events." It includes the building of a primitive campground in, perhaps, the Black Rock Springs area, imposition of individual user fees, and an upgrade of the Visual Resource Management or "VRM" classifications. All of this is pretty much business as usual, the increasing pressure of population forcing the government to channel people into predetermined experiences so they don't trash the environment.

The only new development immediately apparent here are the VRM designations. For years, the government has been seeking to quantify the value of scenery with objective standards. Mike Bilbo and his colleagues have sharpened the leading edge by putting to paper how it could work. In a simplified form, Class 1 means that you leave the landscape almost totally alone; anything you do to it must be very nearly invisible. Class 2 accepts buildings if their look is in character with the natural landscape and they don't attract attention. Class 3 allows for more visible buildings, although they're still supposed to be designed in character with the local landforms. Class 4 accepts major industrial development, the impact of which will inevitably dominate the landscape.

Under Alternative 1, most of the playa would be under Class 2 protection, which would allow the BLM to construct campgrounds and for Burning Man to continue, if it restores the playa to its original condition each year. Class 2 also protects the "viewshed" along which your vision flows out onto the playa, so this alternative would limit development in the surrounding mountains.

Under Alternative 2, which is relatively and deliberately draconian, everything would be made a VRM Class 1, resource development would be banned, and most mechanized travel would be eliminated.

Clearly there's an agenda at work here, the BLM guiding the public toward the preferred Alternative 1, and for the most part it works, a compromise almost everyone accepts with some reservations, Mark and myself included. Mark's comments, however, are significant, and ones that he and I have discussed while traveling together through every state in the Intermountain West, where we've had a chance to examine the results of all three kinds of alternatives.

Terry Reed, before coming to the BLM's Winnemucca Field Office, managed the Imperial Sand Dunes, which are located southeast of the Salton Sea and are a heavily used recreational area that Mat and I visited after Slab City. These are the dunes where San Diego artists associated with the Center for Land Use Interpretation placed the subversive water cooler. It's a fully functional sculpture/performance piece meant to draw attention to an encroaching civilization that installs intrusive amenities, such as the ATM-like fee booth the BLM placed at the entrance, part of its response to the millions of Southern Californians running rampant over the dunes. Money generated in this federally mandated "fee demonstration area" was kept local and used specifically to manage the area.

Although I consider it double taxation, I'm used to paying to use the outdoors, and to some extent I will support local user fees—but the angular machines placed on the edges of the flowing dunes were in such visual disparity with their environment that Mat and I refused to enter the area. It was a visceral reaction to a philosophical conundrum, and one that Mark and Alvin and I experience on an increasing basis as the BLM and other agencies scramble to protect the lands they manage. Terry is aware that the fee booths aren't an ideal solution, but he'd like to "keep ahead of the curve of California." If he can raise money to protect the Black Rock before the hordes arrive, he wants to do so.

Because Mark is concerned with a quality of life that includes open views where the hand of man is not evident, he finds the quantification of visual resources an appealing idea. Where he disagrees with the BLM is in the development of the Black Rock and the institution of fees. Just as the specific scenic value of the playa consists of its unobstructed view of the earth, which the BLM specifically notes in its report, so is its primary experiential value in an unmediated visit. And that runs contrary to business as usual. Erect a sign directing visitors to a campground, for instance, and you run the risk of not only blocking the literal view, but you deprive visitors of finding a place for themselves. Set up water coolers, and you deprive them of the chance to be adults responsible for carrying their own water (exactly the point that the CLUI installation made). You may protect the environment, but in doing so you severely mitigate the ability of humans to rediscover the world, a strategy that Mark believes is beginning to cause enormous resentment in the populace.

"Someone once said 'Build it and they will come,'" observes a woman in the audience. "Well, don't build it, and they won't come!" This comment is popular with the audience, which suspects that fees will only encourage the agency do something with the money, such as construct a campground.

Some scientists would argue that the evolution of our vision is indelibly bound to our need to explore. Expanding populations of hominids have for millions of years made it necessary for us to wander into and reconfigure new terrain for living space, and our vision is both hardwired and programmed to cope with that challenge, which gives us a sense of satisfaction when we do so. Now there aren't any new places to go where people haven't been, but we're still governed by the genetic need to explore. We can meet that need if we leave alone parts of the world for reexploration, for individual rediscovery. Progressively cutting off more and more access to that deeply rooted need can only breed resistance after a certain point.

Mark, Alvin, and I come from three very dissimilar backgrounds, parts of the country, and lifestyles, but we all agree that widespread, long-term grassroots education is the key. If you can teach everyone how to respect the desert—or forests or beaches or buildings—then you don't have to regulate them. If people know to tread lightly on the playa, and to pack out everything they bring onto it, there won't be a need to pave a road across it and funnel them into a campground that eventually would include graffiti-proofed steel tables. The strongest argument that Burning Man can offer in favor of being allowed to continue its operations on the playa, in fact, isn't the hundreds of thousands of dollars it generates for the BLM, or for local businesses. Instead, it's the massive education on desert protocol that it provides the participants, which is probably the largest single such educational program in the country, and one the BLM greatly appreciates. I would argue, in fact, that this is a role model for cooperation between government and the private sector, where education is in everyone's interest and basically paid for by participant fees.

The BLM conscientiously records the comments and urges people to put them in writing on the forms provided. It's obvious that, given unforeseen politics, they're going to adopt the middle-of-the-road Alternative 1—if we're lucky, they'll tweak it to keep fees and development to a minimum. Terry, who seeks out Mark after the meeting, seems genuinely intrigued by the idea of broadening experiential values for the agency beyond the Visual Resource standards, a larger definition Mark thinks could make explicit the need to preserve opportunities for rediscovery in the outdoors.

Mark and I head back to Alvin's house in Reno, a two-hour drive that takes us in under the umbrella of light that the urban area casts outward for miles beyond the city limits. This is the end of my roaming the playas for this year, and I'm melancholy, yet pleased to have found what I think are more threads tying together art and landscape.

One of them has to do with this increasing desire by the government to quantify human appreciation of scenic values, an effort that has been ongoing sporadically since at least the late 1960s and now finds form in the BLM's Visual Resource classes. That we have a widespread need to preserve viewsheds of open landscape is undeniable, and the reason why we do so may be linked to art through our evolution.

Jane Jacobs, one of the most influential writers on the designed environment, points out in *The Nature of Economies* that aesthetic appreciation is a trait shared among humans worldwide and throughout cultures in time. Such a persistent behavioral trait, Jacobs argues, points strongly to its being one not only based in our genetics but tied to the very survivability of the species. To perform a half-Nelson here, one of the "economies of nature" is that species usually don't harbor genes that widespread unless they're there for a purpose. Jacobs believes that aesthetic appreciation may be a trait we've developed in order to help us preserve our habitat.

Species that are successful, by virtue of their rate of reproduction and longevity, tend to consume their ecological niches. Viruses and bacteria can kill off not only their individual hosts but entire populations; goats will eat themselves right off the rangelands; fuel-gathering humans can so strip a landscape of living and fossil vegetation, from trees to coal, that the land is laid to waste for thousands of years. Yet something in our behavior, as well as that in many other species, has forestalled us from doing so everywhere and over time. Jacobs postulates that we have bred into ourselves an appreciation for healthy landscapes in order that we not irrevocably overconsume where we live. Sometimes we define those landscapes as cultivated farmlands or handsome streets, but more often than not it's those unspoiled, pristine, and even sublime landscapes that show up in art. Just as we unconsciously search another person's appearance to judge his or her genetic viability as a partner—the symmetry of features, the strength of protein in hair, and so forth—so we may have genetic predispositions toward admiring and preserving parklands and awe-inspiring landscapes. It may simply be in our own best interest to do so.

That's one thread: that, although we have genes allowing us to compete successfully for resources in the landscape, we may also have genes that help us preserve the landscape, genes that express themselves through aesthetic behavior, a set of linked traits that sometimes are at odds with each other on the surface (loggers versus environmentalists) but at deeper levels are well integrated for our survival overall.

Here's a related proposition: perhaps we deliberately seek out cognitive dissonance in nature. Even if we are uncomfortable in environments in which our mental templates cannot encompass easily and quickly the reality, our intuition about the lay of the land thus failing us, we have for so many millions of years been forced to migrate into and through such spaces as the deserts that we no longer can resist their challenge. We've bred ourselves to survive the difficulties offered by these environments, and now we're addicted to them. We still have trouble making our way around the playas; they're still anomalies within our deep genetic predilection for the woodlands and savanna; but we remember how transcendent we felt when traversing the deserts, our senses, hence our mind, dislocated out of familiarity with the world, and thus admitting of new thoughts.

We seek out cognitive dissonance in art as well. Speaking now just about landscape art, yes, we as a whole prefer the familiar mode developed in southern Europe almost a millennium ago: a shaded foreground framed with trees in which humans are placed before a water feature in the midground, the mountains on the horizon fading into the blue distance. As viewers, we are peering out from the safety of the trees implied by the darkened foreground and the foliage. Some of our own kind are nearby, so it must be safe, and there's water available. And the way the mountains shift away from us in the spectrum tells us how large is the landscape itself, and how we're placed in it. That's our aesthetic appreciation of a landscape fit for human presence, and one that we want to preserve.

Yet we also like to be shaken out of these expectations, these preferences that are so surprisingly clear across so many different cultures and countries. We like to contemplate vigorous abstract works by artists such as Piet Mondrian and Jackson Pollock, or the cool minimalism of Agnes Martin and the hot vibrating optical paintings of Bridget Riley. We want our vision to be challenged, our minds to be stretched.

As I pointed out at the beginning of this book, art is mortal, in some cases nearly 99 percent of what's created in one country disappearing within a few centuries. Far from being dismayed by this, I am instead convinced that if this weren't so, our species would turn psychotic. If we didn't have the visual room, the mental space, in which to freely recreate images of the world and ourselves—be they representational or abstract—if we were hemmed in and surrounded by all of the art of all of the centuries, boredom and claustrophobia would turn us into vicious zombies.

This is, finally, related to the desert in general, and most especially the playas. The more we convert open land into landscape through art, architecture, and memory, the more we need spaces that we have not yet tamed into a familiar place. Just as the slate of art history is swept clean by accidents, war, and just plain entropy—the paint falling off the rotting canvas and the glue of the sculpture letting go—so sun and rain and the great winds restore annually the palimpsest that is the playa.

It's increasingly fashionable to apply our very, very rudimentary knowledge of genetics to all kinds of behavior, from how we raise children to why we have wars and apply patterned colors on flat surfaces. The impulse is understandable, a desire to have rational explanations for what appear to be irrational or nonutilitarian acts; it's also dangerous, because the misapplication of genetics, all too easy at this stage, can be used to justify the most horrific acts and ideas. But just as we profit by understanding the genetic basis for language, so will the parsing out of the relationships among our cognitive evolution, art, and landscape bring us important information about our place in the world.

In the meantime, as Mark pointed out in Gerlach, we need the opportunity to rediscover the world for ourselves, places where we're not guided by interpretative signs and herded into campgrounds. As it is in culture, so it is in nature, the two meeting on the playa, appearing, disappearing, rediscovered by anyone who will go there and look.

Sources

Although a moderately extensive technical literature on playas exists on-line, as a landform the playas remain relatively under-represented in books for laypeople, perhaps a minimalist state of grace befitting a geological palimpsest. Deserts as a geographical category are of course more thoroughly represented in the culture:

Allen, Tony, and Andrew Warren, eds. *Deserts: The Encroaching Wilderness.* New York: Oxford University Press, 1993. A useful and well-illustrated primer on deserts worldwide.

Banham, Reyner. *Scenes in America Deserta.* Salt Lake City: Gibbs M. Smith, 1982. A modern classic of desert literature, the picture inside of the author riding a folding bicycle across the playa of Silurian Lake north of Baker in the Mojave says much. Banham was an expatriate English architectural critic living in Los Angeles when he first explored and then became addicted to the desert. Chief among his virtues is an aversion to hyperbole.

Darlington, David. *The Mojave: A Portrait of the Definitive American Desert.* New York: Henry Holt and Co., 1996. This is a readable and entertaining contemporary introduction to one of the two deserts discussed in this book and contains insightful information about the military presence on it.

Grayson, Donald K. *The Desert's Past: A Natural Prehistory of the Great Basin.* Washington, D.C: Smithsonian Institution Press, 1993. One of two major books about the region, it provides requisite background reading.

Fiero, Bill. *Geology of the Great Basin.* Reno: University of Nevada Press, 1986. Although Fiero has little to say about playas, his copiously illustrated book is an excellent reference. Readers desiring to know more about the awesome complexities of Nevada's geology should also read John McPhee's classic *Basin and Range* (New York: Farrar, Straus and Giroux, 1981).

Houghton, Samuel G. *A Trace of Desert Waters: The Great Basin Story.* Reno: University of Nevada Press, 1994. Originally published in 1976, this remains the layperson's definitive source for information on water in the Great Basin, which is essential to understanding the playas.

Larson, Peggy. *The Deserts of the Southwest.* San Francisco: Sierra Club Books, 1977. A useful primer for how deserts are defined worldwide, and a handy natural history guide to our North American ones.

McGinnes, William G., Bram J. Goldman, and Patricia Paylore, eds. *Deserts of the World: An Appraisal of Research into the Physical and Biological Environments.* Tucson: University of Arizona Press, 1968. Although outdated, this volume of papers commissioned by the U.S. Army is an excellent source book for historical literature on deserts and playas.

McNamee, Gregory. *The Sierra Club Desert Reader.* San Francisco: Sierra Club Books, 1995. An excellent and informative "literary companion" to the volume listed above.

Mifflin, M. D., and M. M. Wheat. *Pluvial Lakes and Estimated Pluvial Climates of Nevada.* Reno: Mackay School of Mines, University of Nevada, Reno, 1979.

Neal, James T. *Playas and Dried Lakes.* Stroudsburg, Penn.: Dowden, Hutchinson and Ross, 1975. This "Benchmark Papers in Geology/

20" is the most frequently cited compendium of major mid-twentieth-century scientific work. While exceedingly technical for the most part, it contains a plethora of facts about playas worldwide.

Rosen, Michael R., ed. *Paleoclimate and Basin Evolution of Playa Systems.* Boulder: Geological Society of America, 1994. As above, a series of technical papers; the editor proposes a new system for the classification of playas based on their relationship to groundwater.

Russell, Israel C. *Geological History of Lake Lahontan: A Quaternary Lake of Northwestern Nevada.* Washington, D.C: United States Geological Survey, 1885. This is the baseline book from which all other descriptions of the Great Basin geophysical region arise.

———. *Quaternary History of the Mono Valley, California.* Lee Vining, Calif.: Artemesia Press, 1984. Russell was the pioneering geologist who first described the scientific circumstances of playas in the West; this is a reprint of his article from the *Eighth Annual Report of the United States Geological Survey, 1889* (pp. 267–94). The mix of exploration and adventure with science and cartographic art is extraordinary.

Steiert, Jim. *Playas: Jewels of the Plains.* Lubbock: Texas Tech University, 1995. Featuring numerous photographs by Wyman Meinzer, the book documents the wetland playas found on the High Plains.

Trimble, Stephen. *The Sagebrush Ocean: A Natural History of the Great Basin.* Reno: University of Nevada Press, 1989. The other major book about the region, illustrated copiously with the author's photographs, it contains a few tidbits about playas.

Two on-line sources of information upon which I relied, led there by Mike and Barbara Bilbo, are the USGS "Ground Water Atlas" at www.water.usgs.gov, and the playa site at Texas Tech University, www.lib.ttu.edu/playa.

Figures on the increasing population of the American Southwest are from Rodger Doyle's article "In a Dry Land," which appeared in the

July 2001 issue of *Scientific American*. News of Lake Chad's retreat was reported by Andrew C. Revikin in the *New York Times* on March 27, 2001.

Historical information regarding Frémont, Preuss, and the emigrations across Nevada can be found in many books, among them:

Cline, Gloria Griffen. *Exploring the Great Basin*. Norman: University of Oklahoma Press, 1963.

Frémont, John Charles. *A Report of the Exploring Expedition to the Rocky Mountains in the Year 1843, and to Oregon and North California in the Years 1843–44*. Washington, D.C.: Sen. Exec. Doc. 174, 28th Cong., 2nd Sess., 1845. The edition of this report that I use is actually the 1970 reprint from the University of Illinois Press edited by Donald Jackson and Mary Lee Spence. All quotes of Frémont are from volume 1 of their two-volume set, *The Expeditions of John Charles Frémont* (Urbana: University of Illinois Press, 1970). Other editions of Frémont's accounts are available, but the map portfolio in this set makes a particularly pertinent one for the purposes of this book.

Goetzmann, William H. *Exploration and Empire: The Explorer and the Scientist in the Winning of the American West*. New York: History Book Club, 1966. This Pulitzer Prize-winning book, along with Goetzmann's earlier *Army Exploration into the American West, 1803–1863*, is an often-quoted reference work. It is particularly valuable in that it contains much information regarding the artists accompanying the expeditions.

Stansbury, Captain Howard. *The Exploration of the Great Salt Lake*. 1852; rprt., Washington, D.C.: Government Printing Office, 1988. Reprinted from the 1852 original government report, this paperback edition contains numerous plates.

Land art and earthworks continue to generate books on an increasingly frequent basis. Selected titles referred to were as follows:

Bourdon, David. *Designing the Earth: The Human Impulse to Shape Nature.* New York: Harry N. Abrams, 1995. A photographic anthology that places earthworks in the context of earth shelters, defensive structures, tombs, and other earthen architecture.

Brown, Julia, ed. *Michael Heizer: Sculpture in Reverse.* Los Angeles: Museum of Contemporary Art, 1984. Still the single most comprehensive reference work on the artist considered to be the father of contemporary earthworks (a term not in favor with the sculptor).

Celant, Germano. *Michael Heizer.* Milan: Fondazione Prada, 1997. A huge picture book on the sculptor's work, it actually contains more photographs of playas than any other book I know.

Kastner, Jeffrey, ed. *Land and Environmental Art.* London: Phaidon Press, 1998. A huge anthology of documentary photographs and statements by the artists, this is currently the largest book on land art.

Sonfist, Alan, ed. *Art in the Land: A Critical Anthology of Environmental Art.* New York: E. P. Dutton, 1983.

The literature on rock art is enormous. Here are three books that examine not only the images but the history of our interpretations of them. Although they concentrate primarily on European rock art, they are relevant to our interpretations of images found in the deserts of the American Southwest:

Bahn, Paul G. *Journey Through the Ice Age.* Berkeley: University of California Press, 1997. In this large picture book for the layperson, Bahn, a world-renowned authority, is a stern critic of almost every theory proposed concerning the intent behind prehistoric images.

Conkey, Margaret W., et al., eds. *Beyond Art: Pleistocene Image and Symbol.* Wattis Symposium Series in Anthropology. Berkeley: University of California Press, 1997. This is a critical anthology of anthropological papers; although technical in nature, the reading is intermittently fascinating.

Lippard, Lucy. *Overlay: Contemporary Art and the Art of Prehistory.* New York: Pantheon Books, 1983. Lippard is an art critic who is known for her useful encyclopedic tendencies. This book, although its anthropology is dated, is no exception and contains numerous photographs of both prehistorical geoglyphs and modern earthworks, as well as ancient rituals that burned wooden figures.

Sources for "A Tour of the Playa" start with the Center for Land Use Interpretation, which can be found on the Internet at www.clui.org. CLUI publications referred to were *Hinterland* (1997); *Route 58* (1997); *Around Wendover* (1998); and of course the incomparable *The Nevada Test Site: A Guide to America's Nuclear Proving Ground* (1996). No authors are listed for these publications, in typical CLUI modesty, but Matthew Coolidge has had more than a little to do with them.

In "A Tour of the Playa, Part I," readers may find Lawrence Weschler's *Mr. Wilson's Cabinet of Wonder* (New York: Pantheon Books, 1995) an interesting introduction to the Museum of Jurassic Technology, though it has been suggested that it may go too far in analyzing the exhibits and thus undoing some of the very mystery that makes the place so special.

The playas of the Mojave, as well as Groom Lake/Area 51, are placed into historical, military, and metaphorical contexts by Phil Patton's intelligent and thorough exploration of post–World War II military "black operations" in the Mojave, *Dreamland* (New York: Random House, 1998).

Several books about Michael Heizer's work are available in addition to the Celant book cited above, but two of particular relevance are the collection of photographs taken by Heizer in *Double Negative: Sculpture in the Land* (New York: Rizzoli, 1991), and a seminal exhibition catalog edited by Julia Brown, *Michael Heizer: Sculpture in Reverse* (Los Angeles: Museum of Contemporary Art, 1984).

Jean Tinguely's adventures out on Jean Dry Lake were supposed to be chronicled by a crew from NBC's *Brinkley Journal*, but the power source for their filming was diverted to set off the explosions, this defeating the original purpose of the staged media event. The happening was covered by the *Las Vegas Sun* (23 March 1962) and more thoroughly by John Flynn writing for the Associated Press in the *Las Vegas Review-Journal* (22 March 1962).

Richard Misrach's photographs of the Mojave and Great Basin deserts can be found in numerous books, the most comprehensive of which is *Crimes and Splendors: The Desert Cantos of Richard Misrach*, curated by Anne Wilkes Tucker, with an essay by Rebecca Solnit. Boston: Bullfinch Press, 1996.

In "A Tour . . . Part II," the DOE/NV-562 (August 1999) publication *Guide to Frenchman Flat* was helpful. An illustrated guide by Derek Scammell to the valley, it is the beginning of what he hopes eventually will be a guidebook to the entire NTS.

Among the numerous books available about deserts and nuclear issues, three were consulted more than others. Rebecca Solnit's *Savage Dreams: A Journey into the Hidden Wars of the American West*, originally published by the Sierra Club, was reissued in paperback by the University of California Press in 2000. A. Constandina Titus has revised her excellent *Bombs in the Backyard: Atomic Testing and American Politics* (1986; 2nd ed., Reno: University of Nevada Press, 2000). *Deserts as Dumps: The Disposal of Hazardous Materials in Arid Ecosystems* is an examination by several scientists of the risks and strategies of storing nuclear materials in deserts. Edited by Charles Reith and Bruce Thomson (Albuquerque: University of New Mexico Press, 1992), it explores why deserts may be better places than others for such storage—but inevitably it also documents how fast our knowledge about nuclear waste disposal evolves.

The Federation of American Scientists maintains a large Website devoted to monitoring nuclear weapons and related matters, which can be found at: www.fas.org.

In "A Tour . . . Part III," readers interested in finding out more about the saltworks can examine *Reilly Industries, Inc.* (no author, no date), a corporate brochure that includes information on Reilly's operations. An anonymous United Press news service article in the *Elko Daily Free Press,* 8 May 1999, that was mounted in the Wendover Visitors' Center provided additional information on the brine-pumping efforts of Reilly Industries. Much of Peter Rock's first novel, *This Is the Place* (New York: Anchor Books/Doubleday, 1997), is set in Wendover. The author, who was born in Salt Lake City in 1967, constructs elegant descriptions and metaphors for the salt flats.

The "Coda" on Owens Dry Lake contains figures pulled from a preliminary article on the Internet by Marith C. Reheis of the United States Geological Survey on "Owens (Dry) Lake: A Human-Induced Dust Problem," which can be found at: http://geochange.er.usgs.gov/sw/impacts/geology/owens.

The town of Keeler is described in Lynn Foster's *Adventuring in the California Desert* (San Francisco: Sierra Club Books, 1987).

While writing about the Smoke Creek Desert and the work of Michael Moore and his predecessors, I found the following helpful:

Alpers, Svetlana. *The Art of Describing: Dutch Art in the Seventeenth Century.* Chicago: University of Chicago Press, 1983. The early and evolving relationships among cartography, coastal profiles, and landscape painting are explored here in this important study with convincing scholarly detail.

Burnside, Wesley M. *Maynard Dixon: Artist of the West.* Provo, Utah: Brigham Young University Press, 1974.

Fox, Cheryl A., ed. *Nevada Historical Society Quarterly* 33, no. 2 (Summer 1990). A special issue on Nevada artists guest-edited by the printmaker and former chairman of the art department at the University of Nevada, Reno, Jim McCormick, it includes rare essays on Craig Sheppard and Robert Caples.

Clark, Walter Van Tilburg. *Robert Cole Caples: A Retrospective Exhibition, 1927–1963.* Reno: University of Nevada Press, 1964. Written from interviews with and letters from Caples, this is a rare and somewhat quirky look at the artist.

Growdon, Marcia Cohn. *Robert Cole Caples: The Artist and the Man.* Reno; Sierra Nevada Museum of Art (now Nevada Art Museum), 1981. This twenty-page catalog from a small exhibition of Caples's work is the only publication about his work of which I am aware.

Hagerty, Donald J. *Desert Dreams: The Art and Life of Maynard Dixon.* Rev. ed.; Salt Lake City: Gibbs-Smith Publishers, 1998. This is currently the definitive monograph on the artist.

McCormick, Jim, and Monique Laxalt. *An Elegant Line: The Art of the Sheppard Family.* Reno: Nevada Museum of Art, 2000. McCormick, who was hired by Sheppard and assumed the chairmanship of the University of Nevada, Reno, art department after he passed away, is a definitive source on Sheppard's life and work.

Wheeler, Sessions S. *Nevada's Black Rock Desert.* Caldwell, Idaho: Caxton Printers, 1978. Still the most popular text about the Black Rock, the book features several paintings by Craig Sheppard reproduced in black and white. Wheeler (1911–1998) wrote several books about the Great Basin desert, including one on Pyramid Lake, all of which are informative sources.

Yochelson, E. L., and C. M. Nelson. *Images of the U.S. Geological Survey, 1879–1979.* Washington, D.C.: USGS, 1983.

The panoramas by von Egloffstein appear in volume 11 of the Congressional publication *Reports of Exploration and Surveys to Ascertain the Most Practicable and Economical Route for a Railroad from the Mississippi River to the Pacific Ocean* (Washington, D.C.: Sen. Exec. Doc. 36th Cong., 2nd Sess., 1861). My thanks to Alvin McLane for letting me spend hours with his copy.

Information about the life of Israel C. Russell, regretfully for whom no biography exists, was gleaned from the Bailey Willis obituary, "Memoir of Israel C. Russell," in the *Bulletin of the Geologic Society of*

America 18 (1908): 582–92; and G. K. Gilbert's "Israel Cook Russell, 1852–1906," in the *Journal of Geology* 14, no. 8 (November–December 1906): 663–67. Lee Regan at the USGS library in Reston, Virginia, contributed a useful entry from the *American National Biography*, vol. 19, ed. John A. Garraty and Marl Carnes (Cambridge: Oxford University Press, 1999).

Three books about J. M. W. Turner that are relevant include, first and foremost, John Gage's learned and useful *J. M. W. Turner: "A Wonderful Range of Mind"* (New Haven: Yale University Press, 1987). Richard Townsend's excellent comparison of Turner and Moran, based on two exhibitions, is *J. M. W. Turner: "That Greatest of Landscape Painters"* (Tulsa, Oklahoma: Philbrook Museum of Art, 1998). The third is a book that has suffered mightily at my hands as I've dissected the geometries of various paintings in it with ruler and pencil: John Walker, *Joseph Mallord William Turner* (New York: Harry N. Abrams, 1983).

The most numerous sources about Burning Man are found by going to www.burningman.com and following your nose. Brad Weiners edited *Burning Man* (San Francisco: Hardwired Books, 1997), a well-known book featuring essays by Bruce Sterling, Larry Harvey, and others, but more helpful are the numerous color photos. Sources regarding the Black Rock Desert appear below:

Bilbo, Barbara. *The Black Rock Desert Landscape*. Winnemucca, Nevada: Bureau of Land Management, 1999. Not an official publication from the agency but a handout by a volunteer geomorphologist extremely knowledgeable about the playa, it contains a short but excellent technical bibliography.

DeBuys, William. *Salt Dreams: Land & Water in Low-down California*. Albuquerque: University of New Mexico Press, 1999. One of the better books about place in American literature, this natural and cultural history of the Salton Sea includes a sharp, funny, and pointed portrait of Slab City. My account of that ad hoc community was also informed by articles from the *Los Angeles Times* and the *San Diego Union-Tribune*. Regarding Leonard Knight and his Salvation Mountain, I specifically relied on the article "Out There" by Doug Adrianson in the *Los Angeles Times*, 18 March 1999.

Reed, Georgia Willis, and Ruth Gaines, eds. *Gold Rush: The Journals, Drawings, and Other Papers of J. Goldsborough Bruff, April 2, 1849– July 20, 1851*. New York: Columbia University Press, 1949.

Smith, Raymond M. *Nevada's Northwest Corner*. Self-published, 1996. Written by a retired city planner and military man, this eccentric and disjointed collection of articles about the Black Rock nonetheless contains some interesting historical anecdotes.

The BLM's *Sonoma-Gerlach and Paradise Denio Management Framework Plan Amendment and Draft Environmental Impact Statement* (Winnemucca, Nevada: Winnemucca Field Office, Bureau of Land Management, August 2000) is the planning document referred to in the Afterword. At just over two hundred pages and illustrated with nineteen photographs and a similar number of maps, it is a valuable reference tool about the Black Rock, despite the sometimes toe-numbing prose. Information on the "playa serpents" was provided in personal communications from Mike Bilbo.

Efforts to quantify landscape values are rooted at least partially in the work of the great Finnish geographer Johannes Gabriel Grano (1882–1956), whose *Pure Geography* (Baltimore: Johns Hopkins University Press, 1997) was a groundbreaking effort to classify landscape features according to human cognition. Elwood L. Shafr Jr. and James Mietz made a preliminary stab at formalizing values for the design of parks in *It Seems Possible to Quantify Scenic Value in Photographs* (Washington, D.C: USDA Forest Service Research Paper NE-162, 1970).

Other works cited or referred to in *Playa Works* are listed below:

Adrianson, Doug. "Out There," in *Los Angeles Times Magazine* (28 March 1999). Article on Slab City.

Jacobs, Jane. *The Nature of Economies*. New York: Modern Library,

2000. At only 190 pages, this is one of the most original and startling books I know of on an idea-per-ounce basis.

Keister, Douglas. *Black Rock: Portraits on the Playa*. Emeryville, Calif.: Fisher Photo Press, 1990. A whimsical collection of photographs using the playa as a stage for props and people.

Schwartz, Gary. "Ars Morendi: The Mortality of Art," *Art in America* (November 1996), 72–75.

And finally, I would refer readers to two earlier books by the author that are relevant. *Mapping the Empty* (Reno: University of Nevada Press, 1999) and *The Void, the Grid, & the Sign* (Salt Lake City: University of Utah Press, 2000). The former discusses contemporary artists working in the Great Basin, while the latter explores more thoroughly how cognitive dissonance, cartography, and rock art collide in the region.

William L. Fox is the author of six works of nonfiction exploring the arid regions of the American Southwest. He spent a season in the Antarctic as a participant in the National Science Foundation's Antarctic Visiting Artists and Writers program, and served as a visiting scholar at the Getty Research Institute to work in its art and cognition program, and as a Lannan Foundation writer-in-residence. He has also published fourteen volumes of poetry including *Reading Sand: Selected Desert Poems, 1976-2000*, published by the University of Nevada Press.